Activists under 30

Youth, Media and Culture Series

VOLUME 7

Activists under 30

Global Youth, Social Justice, and Good Work

Edited by

Shirley R. Steinberg

BRILL

SENSE

LEIDEN | BOSTON

Cover illustration: Photographs used with permission.

The Library of Congress Cataloging-in-Publication Data is available online at http://catalog.loc.gov

ISSN 2542-9329
ISBN 978-90-04-37716-5 (paperback)
ISBN 978-90-04-37717-2 (hardback)
ISBN 978-90-04-37718-9 (e-book)

This book is printed on acid-free paper and produced in a sustainable manner.

To the Youth of Marjory Stoneman Douglas High School, Parkland, Florida, Activists from the #MSDSTRONG Movement, who refuse to allow the senseless destruction of lives facilitated by a government which approves, supplies and endorses the sale and use of semi-automatic and automatic weapons

To Eelco Bart Buitenhuis,
Lover and Partner, Teacher, Artist, Musician, Scholar, Muse,
You are missed beyond words

For my kids' kids…our future
Maci, Luna, Cohen, Hava, Tobias, Seth, Milo Joe, Gabby

Contents

Part 2: Youth Voices

Introduction

Effecting Change, Making a Difference

Celebrating Youth Activism

Shirley R. Steinberg

Modern youth have always been activists. Perhaps they weren't noted or seen as such, but the notion of youth is, in itself, an activist construct. Youth activism wasn't named, certainly not celebrated, but it can be traced to the early days of rock n' roll, to the gyrating movements of dance, to the screaming voices of fans, to the rebel youth of the screen, to the long hair and protest voices of the 1960s, and to the unique ways in which youth insist on dressing, speaking, and making their place in the world. This doesn't mean youth have been appreciated nor celebrated, indeed, I make the argument that young men and women are often ignored, ridiculed, marginalized, and feared... the voices of youth are often discounted.

From Little Adults to Youth

Before the mid-twentieth century, teenagers/youth were not considered a societal group—once a child reached the age of nine or ten in many countries, sh/e was considered a little adult. During the Industrial Revolution, youth became commodities to work in factories, expected to marry young, and replicate the culture, social class, and histories of their parents. Youth from poor or working class backgrounds weren't expected to be educated—their destiny was clear, they would simply replace their parents and sustain the status quo. Modern psychology created a designation for adolescence in the beginning of the twen-

tieth century, and as the field grew, it became apparent that youth were nei-
ther older children nor younger adults, they were unique in being transitional.
With the increase of interest in the psyche and the evolution of scholarship on
child and adolescent development, it became clear that along with the physical
and psychological changes and growth within young men and women, their
attitudinal, social, cultural, and intellectual changes were distinct. When popular culture began to feature youth through literature, film, and ultimately,
television, they became identified with rebellion and cultural change.

Be Independent...No, You Can't Do That

Completely different than children and adults as a cultural group, young
women and men were often identified as attitudinal, emotional, restless, and
ungovernable. Cultural depictions of these non-children/non-adults led to
societal beliefs that youth were too old to be babied, and too young to be
trusted. There is an irony in ways in which parents/caregivers often shep-
herd offspring. Babies are celebrated and every developmental and growth
stage heralded in as a miraculous accomplishment. The first time a infant
rolls over, smiles, sits up, crawls, stands, walks, talks—all of these milestones
are met with amazement, applause and support. The primary years are full of
these accomplishments: little graduations, learning to dress, tie shoes, to read,
write, to ride a bike. Indeed, little girls and boys are often pushed to each new
milestone, with parents/caregivers worried if their little one is a bit "late" in
speaking, walking, or kinetic tasks. Children are encouraged to accomplish
and be independent.

And then youth happens. Applause for growing tasks stops, and rules/
restrictions begin to appear. The child who was encouraged to do everything
on their own grows to want to make decisions and explorations. Growing up
becomes an aim and occupation for youth, and parents/caregivers are often
not equipped nor ready to accept this change. As adolescents grow and mature, they are often considered troublesome, inappropriate, impossible and are
no longer celebrated for growing. Youth are often viewed as suspect, criticized,
problematized, pathologized, and restricted. Tensions between adults and
youth become the primary concern in the home, and the happy, celebratory
job of being a child gives way to a difficult and stressful set of years.

Speaking up and Speaking out

The act of growing up, itself, is a form of activism. It is the ability of a young
person to advocate and champion themselves along with their own decisions,
choices, tastes, and future. In this sense, youth are natural activists. Beginning

with personal activism, they learn to make choices and create their own paths. And once this path is established, youth are free to expand this activism to become societal and, in the case of this book, global.

In 1964, the free speech movement was created in the United States to counter the violence and harassment directed toward students by the police. The movement was spearheaded by Jack Weinberg after his experiences as an activist brought him to the understanding that youth must have a voice. Active in civil rights and later in anti-war and pro-environmental movements, he became a social organizer. Discussing his activism, Weinberg noted:

> I was being interviewed by a newspaper reporter, and he was making me very angry. It seemed to me his questions were implying that we were being directed behind the scenes by Communists or some other sinister group. I told him we had a saying in the movement that we don't trust anybody over 30. It was a way of telling the guy to back off, that nobody was pulling our strings. (Galloway, 1990)

The phrase, *don't trust anybody over 30*, became a rallying call for youth engaged in activism. While this book is not encouraging nor discouraging the mistrust of adults, it celebrates the work and dedication of those activists who are under the age of 30. The age designation stands to remind us of the capabilities and rights that youth have and their abilities to make a difference. It insists that youth should be encouraged and supported as they pave their way to adulthood, that they have an invested and inalienable right to participate in the future. That they *are* the future.

#MSDSTRONG:
Youth Demand Change the Landscape in March for Our Lives

Today's youth have redefined the notion of activism. In March of 2018, millions of youth marched and protested in reaction to gun violence and school shootings. Following the murders of 17 students and teachers at Marjory Stoneman Douglas High School in Parkland, Florida, on February 14, 2018, a groundswell of anger and protest grew from survivors of the shootings. Indeed, within days, students' reactions to comatose politicians who sent their "thoughts and prayers" were loud and insistent. The youth determined that actions would be demanded and would not cease until appropriate legislation was passed and American schools would be safe. Initial reaction to the youth and their demands by government officials was to note that it was "too soon" to discuss school shootings. The youth rejected this absurdity and created a media platform that resonated with not only Americans, but the entire world.

Within days, youth were using social media to reach out and defy the National Rifle Association, the White House, and any lawmakers who refused to acknowledge that automatic weapons should be banned, and that arms registration be standardized and implemented using mental profiles, age, history of domestic abuse, and other markers to prevent guns from being acquired so easily. By mid-March, rallies and marches were organized, culminating on March 24, 2018, when over 800,000 marchers, led by youth, filled the Washington D.C. Mall. A full day of speakers presented their united platform for strong gun control, banning of automatic weapons and the acknowledgment of the importance of school safety. Not one speaker was over the age of 18; the march was organized, led, and effected by youth leaders throughout North America. T. Bosley, a speaker from Chicago noted that "Everyday shootings are everyday problems," and that the U.S. could no longer ignore the over-55,000 gun deaths a year. Edna Chavez from South Los Angeles is a Latina youth organizer; she told the crowd that "I learned how to duck from bullets before I learned to read." Insisting on safe lives and safe schools, the youth noted that race was often ignored in media interviews and conversations on gun violence. Naomi Wadler, eleven years-old, spoke about this: "I'm here to represent the African American girls who don't make the news." Naomi concluded, "People have said I'm the tool of some nameless adult...It's not true."

Over 800 global sister marches and demonstrations were held that day, all referencing and supporting the Washington D.C. march led by the youth of Marjory Stoneman Douglas High School. These historical events have assured us that youth have taken their future in hand, that they will not allow adults to act without incorporating youth voices. This has the mark of the next chapter of youth activism. It is to these youth, to those who have died, and to those who refuse to be the pawns politicians, that this book is dedicated.

This book is about activist youth under the age of 30 who self-actualized into becoming changemakers and advocates in a world that often overlooks or ignores their voices. It is about identifying complications, tragedies, and inequalities created and maintained by adults. It is about youth voices insisting on being seen and heard, and demanding and creating solutions. It is a book about community, collaboration, ingenuity, and bravery. It is a book that gathers stories and actions of youth to speak to teachers, parents, and politicians about the need to include youth voices in decision-making.

It is also a collection of biographies of international youth activists. Their stories serve as a backdrop to creating a new history that includes the accomplishments and endeavors of youth. By including a collection of writings by youth, discussing their work, their ideas, and their futures, I intend this to be

an example of how research, study, and decisions about youth can be made…
by including them. This book is a celebration of the future we have when we
support and engage in facilitating youth empowerment.

> I have a dream that this is enough, that this should be a gun-free world,
> PERIOD. "We are going to be a great generation. Say it like you really mean
> it. — Yolanda Renee King, nine years-old (Granddaughter, Martin Luther
> King and Coretta Scott King)

References

Galloway, Paul (1990, Nvember 16). Radical Redux. Chicago Tribune. Tempo/Section 5.
    pp. 1–2.
March for Our Lives. (2018). Quotes from youth speakers. Washington, D.C.: March 24,
    2018.

*Shirley R. Steinberg, Research Professor of Critical Youth Studies, University of
Calgary, Calgary, Alberta, Canada*

Part 1

Global Youth Activists

Chapter 1

Abdel Rahman Alzorgan, Jordan

Saving Water in Jordan

Revital Zilonka

> I dream of a world where people chose the right thing even if they fear the change that comes with it. — Abdel

This is the story of Abdel, a young student from Jordan, who together with his brother, invented a device to collect water and redistribute it the crops to make sure that the crops do not freeze during the cold season. Born in Jordan in 1990, Abdel is a mechanical engineer student in Tafila, Jordan and is an environmental entrepreneur. With his brother, he invented a combined system that deals with irrigation and anti-frost to help their farming family members.

Jordan, a country located in the Middle East, is an Arab kingdom. Its official name is Hashemite Kingdom of Jordan. It's a constitutional monarchy, ruled by a king (Abdullah II) and a parliament with a prime minister at its head. Jordan became independent back in 1946. The Jordanian kingdom was ruled by British mandate right after World War I and for decades was subordinated to the British Empire, although the local leadership retains some autonomy.

In 1947, the population of Jordan was only 450,000 people. In 1948, after the establishment of neighboring Israel, 500,000 Palestinian refugees arrived in Jordan. By 2010, an about 1.9 million Palestinian refugees live in Jordan. During both wars in Iraq, about 500,000 Iraqi refugees arrived to Jordan, and in the past couple of years, thousands of refugees came from Syria due to its civil war. Nowadays, about 9.5 million people live in Jordan (estimation, November 2014).

The large number of refugees in Jordan contributes to its poverty rates and affects the country's economy. The semi-arid weather affects the agriculture in the country and the water crisis we witness in the world influences many countries; one of the phenomenon is a process called desertification, when a land experiences drought and embodies the characteristics of a desert due to climate changes. The unemployment rates in Jordan are about 13% (2012), although a less conservative analysis estimate the real rate as 25% unemployment.

When it comes to education, UNESCO (United Nations Educational, Scientific and Cultural Organization—a United Nations organization dedicated to education, science and culture) ranks Jordan's education system 18th out of 94 countries for providing gender equality in education. The literacy rate in Jordan is 97% among adults (2013) and Jordan has 10 public universities, 16 private universities and 54 community colleges. Also, other good news about Jordan comes from the Global Innovation Index (2011) that ranked Jordan as the third most innovative economy in the Middle East. The first countries were the very rich Qatar and the United Arab Emirates.

Due to Jordan's environmental issues, it receives international aid money to help it cope with crucial issues, such as water, energy and agriculture. Water is an ongoing issue in Jordan, as it is in other countries around the world.

Abdel Rahman Alzorgan started his "on-stage" activism back in 2007, when he was 17 years old. His sister Safaa, while being an undergraduate student (currently she is working on her master's degree in English Literature), was part of a group that wrote and performed comedy skits in her academic institution. His sister introduced him to the group and its cause—to raise money for orphan houses in Jordan—and Abdel joined them. The group became a hit; hundreds of people came to see them every time they performed.

The comedy group did more than raise money for the orphan houses: they raised social awareness among their community. The group of six performers performed shows and plays about political issues, such as the elections, the economy and the education system in the country. They all wrote their skits together and performed it at the university theater. Abdel remembers that in a theater that can hold 150 people, about 300 came to watch their comedy every time they performed—they were very popular. Humor, as we can learn from Abdel's experience, can connect people to causes. The comedy group's shows ran for a duration of five years.

Abdel's family moved from Tafila to Amman back in 2011. His father is an imam in a mosque, and his mother is an Arabic language teacher. He has four siblings: Safaa, the oldest (the one that introduced him to the comedy group), his brother Mohammad, another sister named Doaa and the youngest brother, Nooraldeen.

When he was in sixth grade (13 years old), Abdel had an idea how to conserve water and apply an irrigation system to his family's crops. One day he came home from school, and wrote his idea on a piece of paper. The idea came from a need: Abdel's family and all of his uncles are farmers; they farm wheat and chickpeas. At that time, the season was very dry and the land didn't get enough rain. Most of the crops were lost, and what was left was sold to the shepherds so they could feed the sheep with the ruined crops. "It was a very rough year," Abdel recollects, and that was the first time he had thoughts on how to fix the challenges the farmers were facing. He came up with the idea of how to manage the least amount of water to yield the best crops. Abdel's brother, Muhammad (then 12 years old; nowadays he works for NASA), joined him to develop his vision. His brother came up with an additional idea, regarding an anti-frost system and together they developed a combined system that dealt with irrigation and anti-frost. Abdel worked with his brother on this system throughout his year in tenth grade.

The Alzorgan brothers designed a combined system including an automatic sprinkler system combined with water tanks, a soil moisture sensor and a temperature sensor. On top of these components, the brothers added an alarm system to alert the farmers if their attention was needed, and a control unit. The system sounded alerts in cases of dryness or frosting conditions. The system is also environmentally friendly—it is designed to consume minimum energy and water. In 2006, they applied for the first time to the Intel ISEF (Intel International Science and Engineering Fair) competition—an international science and engineering fair hosted in the USA. That year, the competition was hosted in Indiana. Because the Alzogrgan brothers couldn't speak English, they had a translator from Algeria to accommodate their linguistic needs. Unfortunately, ten minutes before the judging session, the translator had to leave because of an emergency issue in his family. Because of that, the Alzorgan brothers' invention couldn't be judged that year. The brothers went back home to Jordan and decided to learn English. Abdel says, "We learned English from TV. We watched movies and the news in the English language."

In 2008, they went back to compete with their system. That year the competition was held in Atlanta, Georgia, and they won fourth place.

Abdel started his studies majoring in chemistry but then he received a scholarship from King Abdullah II and he switched his major to mechatronic engineering. When he is not in class, he volunteers on campus with the NGO Injaz (www.injaz.org.jo), a group focusing on youth education and developing programs to enhance entrepreneurship, employment opportunites, and career guidance among young students. Nowadays, his activism is mostly involved with overseeing courses offered to the students, and offers help if needed.

When asked what inspires him in life, Abdel replied: "Change. The need to innovate and make life easier and more enjoyable. We are here for a reason, and it's not only about me, or my family and my friends only," he says. His dream is to build a company that will not contaminate the earth like many corporations do. He dreams of affordable solutions for hardworking people. "I dream of a world where people chose the right thing even if they fear the change that comes with it," he explains.

Abdel is a project ambassador for the One Young World organization in Jordan. As the ambassador, he works on implementing international initiatives in Jordan. One Young World (www.oneyoungworld.com) is an international organization operating in London, UK. The organization assists to gather bright minds from all around the world, aged 18–30 years old. The selected young leaders become ambassadors in their countries. Abdel participated in the 2012 One Young World summit in Zurich, Switzerland, and since then he has led some community projects in his country. In 2012, his leadership was recognized by Youth Services America and he was recognized by the organization as one of the world's 25 most powerful and influential young people of that year.

Abdel's advice to young activists is to not get held down due to disappointment. "You need to try and try and try and try until it works," he says. Another important thing he wants to address to young activists is to trust people by getting to know them and their nature, and not by what the media says about them. Abdel thinks that reading is very beneficial because it opens one's mind and will provide more ideas. When one keeps an open mind, one will find a way to implement her or his idea. Also, Abdel stresses, "never reject a person just because of her or his race, color or belief."

Quick Links

• About water and the global water crisis: http://water.org

- Information about the weather and environment in Jordan at King Hussein's website:www.kinghussein.gov.jo/geo_env.html
- Jordanian Friends of Environment: www.jofoe.org
- The Jordanian Environment Society: www.jes.org.jo
- The Water Project: http://thewaterproject.org
- United Nations Environment Programme regarding Jordan's Green Economy: www.unep.org/greeneconomy/AdvisoryServices/Jordan/tabid/56335/Default.aspx

Revital Zilonka, University of North Carolina, Greensboro, Tel-Aviv, Israel

Chapter 2

Anoka Primrose Abeyrathne, Sri Lanka

The Generous Tree of Sri Lanka

Revital Zilonka

Anoka Primrose Abeyrathne is an environmental activist, co-founder and executive director of the Sustain Solutions organization. She is also a lawyer and is currently working toward her master's degree in development studies. Known for the Mangrove Trees Project, a community-based environmental initiative to plant mangrove trees in Sri Lanka to restore the ecosystems in the island damaged by the tsunami in 2004. The Sustain Solution organization also advocates for youth development and trains young students to develop skills in order to assist them to successfully situate themselves in the workforce and in academia.

Anoka Abeyrathne, from Sri Lanka, was born in July 21, 1991. The first time she volunteered was when she was about ten years old. She was part of the Young Zoologists Association in Sri Lanka and did voluntary work related to protecting the environment and animal life.

On December 26th, 2004, a brutal and horrific tsunami hit the Indian Ocean following an earthquake. Sri Lanka was one of the countries that suffered significant damage. The tsunami, caused by the earthquake, killed an estimated 230,000 (185,000 confirmed and 45,000 are stilled declared as missing) people, one-third of them were children. Anoka lost family members in that fatal event. From *Wikipedia:*

The earthquake, with a magnitude of 9.1–9.3, was the third-largest earth-quake ever recorded on a seismograph and one of the most devastating earthquake ever in recorded history. The energy of this earthquake was equivalent of 10,000 nuclear bombs. It had the longest duration of faulting ever observed, between eight and 10 minutes. The earthquake was so intense it caused the entire earth to vibrate 0.4 inches and later triggered other earthquakes as far away as Alaska. Indonesia was the worst affected country in this disaster and has lost the highest number of people (about 170,000). Among the thousands of people that lost their lives in the tsunami, 9,000 foreign tourists, mostly from Europe, died as well. About 1.7 million people lost their houses and were displaced due to the tsunami, most of them from Indonesia and India. That year, many Christmas celebrations around the world were cancelled due to the tragedy, and many countries sent money and medical aid to the affected countries hit by the enormous waves. (Wikipedia, 2018)

Influenced by the impact of the tsunami, Anoka recognized the immense destruction it had caused; she wanted to help the people in her country and decided to joined aid groups to restore her beloved country. "Volunteering was definitely a part of my life, it is also a part of our culture in Sri Lanka where giving to the less fortunate has been ingrained since childhood," she recollects, and explains that she comes from a family that does a lot of volunteer work in their communities.

Sri Lanka is an island country in the northern Indian Ocean off the southeast coast of India. Its population is 21.8 million people (according to the July 2014 census). The most popular religion in Sri Lanka is Buddhism (73%). Other religions in the country are Hindu (11%), Islam (8%) and Christianity (6%). Colombo is the biggest city in Sri Lanka, and it is where Anoka was born, raised and currently lives. The official languages spoken in Sri Lanka are Sinhala and Tamil and English is widely spoken (although it is not an official one). Sri Lanka was colonized by the UK until February 1948 and then established its independence after the British withdrew. The local economy is based on agriculture and its main crops are tea, coconut, rice, and rubber produced from tropical trees. Since the economy is based on agriculture, the earthquake and the tsunami harmed the villagers intensely.

From 1983 to 2009, there was a civil war between the government and the Tamil Tigers, a group that fought to create an independent Tamil state in the north and east of the island. The military defeated the Tamil Tigers and the war ended on May 17th, 2009. The civil war caused the loss of an estimated 80,000–100,000 people. It also came with an economic cost—about $200 million USD was spent on the war over the course of 25 years.

At the age of 13, when the tsunami struck the island, Anoka, as many other young Sri Lankans, became a part of the Mangrove Trees Project. As a young activist already active in environmental issues in her country, Anoka read about the mangrove trees and how they can be a barrier against natural disasters. She convinced her friends to plant some mangrove seedlings with her. As a student, she took biology classes and read more about mangrove trees and researched better ways to replant them. More and more people joined the cause and invested in this project with their own funds. Soon it became a local movement in Sri Lanka, especially since the memory of the tsunami was still fresh for so many. The research showed more reasons to why mangroves are important to the Sri Lankan environment, especially since it is a tiny island in the Indian Ocean battered by waves. The project spread from the Colombo district to other areas and the project had many school children involved, as well as other youth groups and many others from around the island.

The Mangrove Trees Project did not require much money—they had seedlings to initiate the project, and later when they needed more plants, they asked villagers to be involved in the project. The villagers collected the seedlings and prepared them for planting around the island. Later, the British Council, the Commonwealth, Disney and Youth Service America helped fund the project. The project received grants to continue working with youth. Without considering the volunteers and other costs, roughly 10 million in Sri Lankan rupees were collected to maintain the Mangrove Trees Project (about $77,000 USD). $77,000 to save one's beloved country does not sound like much, but it tells of the low cost of living in Sri Lanka. As the tsunami caused significant damage to many ecosystems all around the Indian Ocean, replanting mangrove trees are a crucial and important task to help revive and rehabilitate the local ecosystem.

Mangroves are very special because of their ability to survive in partially saline water. They provide shelter and breeding for many species both birds and fish, as well habitats in the Sundarbans for the threatened species of Bengal tigers. Their roots purify water and balance out acidity, and the tree leaves help ensure the soil is fertile. The fruit can be consumed by birds and humans, and some food and juices are also made with them. The bark and wood are used in traditional craftmaking. The mangrove trees are also one of the biggest carbon capturing systems on the planet. A small area of mangroves is able to capture more than 1,800 kilograms (about 4,000 pounds) of carbon dioxide by helping to clean the polluted air and then deposits the waste in their trunks. Since the mangrove trees thrive in half-saline/half-pure water, they can be usually found near lagoons and estuaries (places where pure water rivers meet the saline water seas and/or oceans). They also require a lot of mud to prosper.

The Mangrove Trees Project still exists. It is being expanded into a social enterprise to make sure it can sustained by the people. The project is being supervised by an organization named Sustain Solutions, an organization Anoka has founded with her friend, Akila Suvin. The project's name is called Growin' Money, and Anoka is in charge of training the people to maintain it in Sri Lanka and neighboring countries in the area of the Indian Ocean.

"The organization was formed in around 2005 to make sure that we had a body to work under more efficiently," Anoka explains. Anoka's partners are Akila, Dilini, Fioni and Kalana—her long-lasting childhood friends. They have been working in half a dozen countries permanently while contributing through consultancies. Recently they were put into the UN World Economic Forum's Sustainable Development Council to work on sustainable policy and the SDGs (Sustainable Development Goals—a UN platform. You can read more about it here: http://sustainabledevelopment.un.org/?menu=1300).

Sustain Solutions is a youth-led organization. They have partners in 23 countries around the world and work on environmental protection, environmental policy, social enterprise and youth-capacity building as well as the promotion of young people. Instead of joining an existing organization, they decided to start a new one because they wanted to be impartial, unbiased and to ensure they did their work in the best way possible with the least amount of bureaucracy. Sustain Solutions has teams in India, Bangladesh, Cambodia and Maldives.

The organization is led by the youth that make up the board of directors and the core team. The volunteers range from the age of 10 to 29. For anyone over 30 years old, the organization has consultancy positions. Anoka stresses that although people over the age of 30 are welcome to contribute to the organization and its functions, but the age of those sitting on the board of directors will always be under the age of 30.

Anoka has an undergraduate degree in law she has received from the University of London in the UK. She is a lawyer and part of her work is to create lawsuits that bring companies and corporations to court. In the past, the organization had issues with corporations trying to cut down mangrove trees for their factories and hotels. Because the mangrove trees grow everywhere and their roots protrude from the water, they block some of the hotels' view of the water. Because of this, the hotel owners wanted to cut them. Sustain Solutions retained some environmental lawyers on behalf of the residents of the area and created a citizen rights lawsuit because the destruction of the water quality that may result from the cutting of the mangroves would affect everyone. However, Anoka and the organization have successfully saved the mangroves. Anoka believes that corporations need to change their business models from focusing only on making a profit to caring about the planet. She gives the Levi's company as an example: they started to manufacture jeans from recycled plastic that are sold for $60 a pair (http://explore.levi.com/news/sustainability/introducing-levis-wasteless-8-bottles-1-jean).

As mentioned, Anoka got her degree in law "…because it would be the easiest way to influence policy. I wanted to be a vet or a doctor when I was younger, but thought that instead of helping just a few, through law I could help a lot more people." She chose to pursue a law degree in the UK because the legal system is very similar to that in Sri Lanka. Currently, she is pursuing a master's degree in the University of Colombo in Sri Lanka, in development studies. Her curriculum includes public law, international law, administrative law, common law, land law and other legal issues.

One of the key components in Anoka's activism is having a support system. She describes her family as a great one. Her parents always let her do what she wanted to do and supported her goals and aspirations. "I was brought up very differently from other girls in Sri Lanka because they are taught to be so afraid of doing anything different. So my friends and family have always been helpful and understanding and non-judgemental, which has been the best support," she explains. One of her mentors is Thushara Gunasekera from the British Council: "She is an amazing lady who took me under her wing when I was 18 years old and taught me so much about life, compassion and generosity. Another would be Alain Sibenaler who is the current United Nations Population Fund representative in Sri Lanka as well as Nishantha and Jayan from the UN in Sri Lanka. I have also an amazing mentor in the form of Asanga Abeygoonasekera who has been immensely supportive while Lisa Habersack from the IYF is a brilliant mentor." Anoka is also inspired by other activists around the world, such as Wangari Mathai from Kenya, Aung San Sukyi from Burma, the late Gandhi (India) and Dr. Martin Luther King Jr. (USA).

In her role at Sustain Solutions, she is the executive director and co-founder. Her day typically starts at 4 AM. She does her exercise and/or yoga and then go on to work for two hours after which she heads to the mangrove sites or university. Then, she meets villagers, stakeholders or other organizational bodies interested in working with the organization. She also works on developing the programs involving youth so they will have more knowledge on capacity-building and social enterprise. Sustain Solutions provides training in IT skills, personal skills-building, presentation skills and advocacy skills.

Anoka and her organization recognize that the Sri Lankan education system does not meet the youth's needs. Although the education system is free, it does not prepare the students for life. High-schoolers that come from the rural areas in the country and get accepted to college do not have any knowledge of the English language and IT skills. Sustain Solutions provides these young students opportunities such as internships in companies so they can live up to their full potential. The organization implements educational components in the programs they provide, and are currently working with the Ministry of Education on creating a more eco-focused education. "We do hands-on work at the grassroots level as well," Anoka explains. Her day does not end when she gets back home at 6 PM—then, she continue to work on her studies and the organization's work plan, as well as on strategic plans for the upcoming year.

With this type of daily schedule, it is no wonder she has received so many awards in her life so far, and was recognized by many worldwide organizations for her amazing activism. Among her accomplishments, we can count her role as a *Global Youth Ambassador* (2014), *Commonwealth Youth Award* (2013) for excellence in development work, *Global Changemaker* (2011) from the British Council and the *SAARC Youth Award* (2010) for outstanding contribution to the protection of environment and mitigation of climate change, and was recognized as an *International Climate Champion* by the British Council in 2010 (when she was 19 years old).

Anoka does not get paid for the Mangrove Trees Project. She wants all the funds go directly to the project. To support herself financially, she does some consultancy work and practices as a lawyer. She still lives with her parents so her expenses are low. For fun, she does a lot of hiking, driving and traveling. As a role model in her community, Anoka mentors youth. Her advice to young activists is to "not let anyone stop you from following your heart and to always do the best possible to make your journey on earth an amazing one that leaves the planet and everyone around you in a better state." She adds: "I believe that when you do something from your heart, it always goes well."

Quick Links

- www.wikihow.com/Become-an-Activist
- http://sustainsolutions.wordpress.com/2014/06/15/how-to-go-green-right-now
- www.sustainsolutions.org
- http://sustainsolutions.wordpress.com

- www.naturia.per.sg/buloh/plants/mangrove_trees.htm
- www.explorebiodiversity.com/habitats/mangroves.html
- www.americanforests.org/magazine/article/mangroves-in-the-mist
- www.unep.org
- www.tsunami2004.net
- http://academic.evergreen.edu/g/grossmaz/HELGESTJ
- http://en.wikipedia.org/wiki/2004_Indian_Ocean_earthquake_ and_tsunami#mediaviewer/File:2004_Indian_Ocean_earthquake_-_ affected_countries.png
- http://en.wikipedia.org/wiki/2004_Indian_Ocean_earthquake_and_ tsunami

Revital Zilonka, University of North Carolina, Greensboro, Tel-Aviv, Israel

Chapter 3

Charlene Carruthers, US

African American Youth Activist

Venus Evans-Winters

My vision for freedom is bigger than prison cells, drones, privatized education, state surveillance, and it's large enough for us all to live with dignity.
This vision, rooted in the dreams of my ancestors and lessons from my parents and love for my people, carries me through the challenges and weight
of a system set up to commodify and violate my humanity. — Charlene
Carruthers

Charlene Carruthers is an African American woman youth organizer. She
self-defines as a radical Black feminist, "who holds radical values, aimed at
queering political analysis and movement practice." Her inspirational words in
the opening quote above provide insight into her vision for her country and all
of humanity. The words above also suggest where and how Charlene has developed her keen leadership style and committed to social justice endeavors. Charlene's vision for her country and her leadership practices are derived from her
family and community, as well as knowledge of commitment of African American women, among others, to combating race, class, and gender inequality.

All activists have a social and philosophical framework that informs their
vision of the world. Radical Black feminism is the framework that informs
Charlene's vision of the world in which she lives. Black feminism as an ideol-
ogy and practice informs her political work and how she locates herself within
systems of power in the social world. As she asserts, Black feminism requires

her to "seek different understandings and build new spaces." As a Black feminist, she also recognizes the varied histories of Black women in the Diaspora. Politically, she asserts the need for an anti-imperialists/anti-capitalist praxis. In the discussion to follow, we provide a look into Charlene Carruthers' background as a child, her schooling experiences, and her work as a young activist and youth advocate.

Humble Beginnings

Charlene was born and raised in Chicago, Illinois, located in the U.S. Chicago is the third largest city in the country. The city boasts the second oldest transit system in the nation, and is home to the Chicago Bears football team, one of the founding franchises of the National Football League, and is known as the home of jazz, blues and soul music. Chicago is also the former home to one of the world's greatest basketball players, Michael Jordan, media mogul Oprah Winfrey, and former U.S. President Barack Obama. Interestingly enough, the state of Illinois was the first state in the U.S. to ratify the 13th Amendment of the Constitution and abolish slavery.

Undoubtedly, Charlene was influenced by her city's cultural history and state's commitment to civil rights. Despite the fact that Charlene's city and state are well-known around the world for its rich cultural diversity, arts, corporations and industrialized economy, Charlene grew up in and attended school in the city's toughest neighborhoods, known as the Englewood district, located on the south side of Chicago. Although rich with African American heritage and culture, Englewood's African American neighborhoods have a long tradition of experiencing economic and political neglect from city officials. Today, the residents of Chicago face the following social issues:

- Forty to 60 percent of Chicago's south and west side residents live below the poverty line;

- In 2013, nearly 50 public schools were closed in lower-income neighborhoods;

- Illinois ranks dead last in the nation in school funding;

- Chicago has a 7.4 percent unemployment rate;

- Ninety-two percent of Black male teens are unemployed;

- At 19 percent, African-American unemployment in Chicago ranks the third highest in the country;

- 22,144 students were homeless in the 2013–14 school year; and

- Seventy-nine percent of Chicago police youth arrests were African American youth.

Unfortunately, African American and lower-income families are most impacted by inequalities in housing, employment, and education. Furthermore, African American youth, in particular younger men, are victims of police harassment and brutality. While growing up, Charlene avoided the pitfalls too many of Englewood youth faced, such as early pregnancy, alcohol and drug abuse, or death due to violence, by focusing on her family's and teachers' messages that education was the vehicle to change her individual circumstance and the African American community. Her parents also discussed with her the importance of respecting all people. "My parents taught me the value of education and respecting all people regardless of where they come from. I've carried that with me my entire life," explains Charlene.

Charlene, of course, carried these values forward with her from home and community to college and her professional career as an activist. Her long-term objectives are to help improve the city of Chicago, and the quality of life of the most vulnerable children and families in the city and nation. Another goal is to prepare other young people to become advocates and change agents for themselves and others.

Education and Knowledge
After successfully completing high school, Charlene received a scholarship to attend Illinois Wesleyan University where she studied history and international studies. It was at Illinois Wesleyan where she further developed a political consciousness and strategies for effecting change. Being the first in her family to attend college student at a private university in the Midwest at times felt isolating for her and other students of color. Charlene joined various student organizations and organized student meetings to demand that the university provide all students, regardless of gender, race/ethnicity, or financial condition access to resources, extra- and co-curricular activities, and courses needed to meet their developmental needs as students.

Her efforts on campus and in the classroom eventually earned her recognition on campus as a discernible student leader. Also, while at Illinois Wesleyan University, Charlene was initiated and became a member of Delta Sigma Theta Sorority, Inc., which is a service sorority of predominately Black college-educated women with chapters in the United States, England, Japan (Tokyo and Okinawa), Germany, the Virgin Islands, Bermuda, the Bahamas, Jamaica and Korea. Following in the legacy of other college-educated Black women of her sorority, Charlene became even more dedicated to community and social change through service and political engagement.

After earning her B.A. degree, Charlene decided to attend graduate school and study social policy. For graduate school, she attended the prestigious and elite Washington University in St. Louis, Missouri, and received a Masters of Social Work degree. In the following, Charlene explains how formal education and training has influenced her activists' ideals and efforts:

> Formal education has taught me that life experiences are informed by actions taken long before I was born. I can remember high school teachers and college professors lecturing about the importance of reading and writing. My ability to communicate through the written word and interpret text has opened my mind up to worlds, thoughts, analysis, ideas and people I would have otherwise been closed off to.

The activist continues and explains below that at times formal schooling is not always in alignment with an activist's schedule; however, through education there is much to be learned about how power works in the world.

> Formal education has also taught me that many of those who teach and write the texts students read are complicit in the oppression of my people. I have an understanding of what forms the consciousness of white and middle-upper Americans because of formal education. I also have an understanding of what many Black Americans rarely have access to given the structure of dominate public education and anti-Blackness and misogyny found throughout many academic disciplines. This makes me a sharper and more strategic organizer, and fuels my desire to read more from revolutionary thinkers.

Because Charlene has experienced schooling as an African American woman, she certainly understands that formal education can be simultaneously a tool of oppression (e.g. supports the values and ideas of the dominating culture) or a tool of liberation (e.g. provides access and information on other revolutionary thinkers and activists). Since completing graduate studies, Charlene has worked on national and grassroots campaigns. She is a political organizer with a specific interest in immigrant rights, economic justice and civil rights. In her current role as the first national coordinator of the Black Youth Project (BYP) 100, she gives attention to racial justice, feminist and youth leadership development to facilitate and encourage youth-led social change. Youth Activism & Advocacy

According to the BYP 100 website, this phenomenal youth activist has led several grassroots and digital strategy campaigns for national progressive organizations including the Center for Community Change, the Women's Media Center, ColorOfChange.org and National People's Action. Further, she has facilitated and developed political trainings for organizations including the National Association for the Advancement of Colored People (NAACP), the Center for Progressive Leadership, the New Organizing Institute, MoveOn.org, Young People For and Wellstone Action. She has also appeared on several national news shows to discuss how violence, poverty, and other forms of inequality impacts youth's positive development and well-being.

Recently, the young activist has returned to her native home of Chicago. When asked why did she decide to return to Chicago, especially since the city has recently experienced tough economic times, especially for African Americans. She responded:

> I sat in New York City for months watching and reading news about Chicago. The Chicago teachers strike agitated me to a point where I had to do something outside of tweeting and having conversations to debunk the dominant narrative of pathological violence among Black people in Chicago. I knew that the city of Chicago and those who have held power over the past several decades have consistently devalued Black life. I came back home to join efforts working against oppressive systems and to create new spaces for our people.

Charlene emphasizes that mentors have played an important role in her development and identity as an activist. In her words, "Being able to see what I wanted to become in real time was more than inspirational—it allowed me to not just think of my goals as dreams, but as an attainable reality." Like most youth activists, Charlene reminds younger and older people of the importance in seeking guidance and advice from those individuals who inspire us and help to build our character. All potential and aspiring youth activists should involve mentors in their life goals.

Historical Legacy

When asked, "Which historical figures do you most identity with?" Charlene named, Harriet Tubman, Ida B. Wells, Shirley Chisholm, and Thomas Sankara. All of these historical figures greatly influenced U.S. politics and culture and are very important civil servants and social justice advocates. For example, Harriet Tubman was a former slave known for helping many enslaved Africans escape to the North to freedom via the Underground Railroad. Over a ten-year span, it is believed that Harriet Tubman made 19 trips into the American South and escorted over 300 enslaved people to freedom. Like

Charlene Carruthers and Harriet Tubman, Ida B. Wells may also be described as a hero of her time.

Ida B. Wells was an African American journalist, newspaper editor, and suffragist. As an early leader of the civil rights movement, Ida B. Wells risked her life speaking out publicly and writing against the lynching of Black people in the U.S. She became known as the mother of the anti-lynching campaign. Some might say that Charlene is similar to Ida B. Wells because as a youth organizer, she has put herself on the front line to speak out against the mass killings of young African Americans at the hands of White adults in contemporary times, in places like Chicago, New York, and St. Louis.

Not surprisingly, Charlene also mentioned that Shirley Chisholm and Thomas Sankara are two historical figures she admires. Shirley Chisholm was an American politician, educator, and author. In 1968, Chisholm became the first African American woman elected to the U.S. Congress. In her political work, Chisholm has been honored for her role in the fight for women's rights, fair wages for workers, and striving to improve the quality of life and opportunities for inner-city residents.

Once a anti-imperialist freedom fighter, Thomas Sankara later became the president of Burkina Faso. With a political focus on African independence, Sankara campaigned for literacy programs, women's health rights, and vaccinations for children. Politically, Sankara has been described as a Marxist revolutionary and Pan-Africanist. There is little doubt that with Charlene's interest in protecting the rights of women and the poor that she has a lot in common with these historical political activists.

Considering Charlene came from humble beginnings and engaged in organized resistance efforts prior to the age of 30, most have already concluded that the youth organizer is already on the path to fostering meaningful world change. Even more importantly, she is passing the social justice torch onto future world leaders as she works diligently to prepare other youth for organized struggle against racism, sexism, and classism. As Charlene has stated:

> When we act collectively with values based in love, our power can grow and transform. No one will give us permission to lead; we just have to do it despite any fear that may be present.

Without a doubt, Charlene Carruthers is a modern-day role model for African Americans, young women and young people around the world.

Reference

Evans-Winters, V. Personal interviews with Charlene Carruthers.

Venus Evans-Winters, Illinois State University, Normal, Illinois USA

Chapter 4

Luis Fernando Cruz, US

Activist for Differently Abled People

Laura Mooney

Imagine not having control of your arms such that typing, texting, and writing are impossible; your voice box does not work either. Now imagine wearing glasses that send what your eyes are looking at to a computer screen. Luis Cruz makes communication technology affordable for those who need it most.

In the Unites States alone, roughly 5.5 million people have some degree of paralysis that affects their ability to control arm and hand movements and to communicate using their voice. Many use head wands or mouth sticks to operate computers or electric wheelchairs, but these devices are often cumbersome and slow. Alternate hands-free communication technology exists, such as eyeball-tracking computer interfaces, but it costs US $10,000 or more to purchase the software and camera equipment required. These costs—just to use a computer for school or to Facebook or email with friends—are significantly out of reach for many individuals with motor or speech difficulties. This is especially problematic in developing countries where US $10,000 is equivalent to several years of an adult's average full-time salary. Luis has figured out a way to put this costly eye-tracking technology into a regular pair of eyeglasses and sell the entire do-it-yourself package for less than US $200. His invention of this low-cost "Eyeboard" won international recognition for innovative technologies and Luis continues to capture worldwide attention as an up-and-coming entrepreneurial heavyweight.

Luis knows he does not have the resources in his home country to continue developing and refining the Eyeboard, so he purposely markets his invention as an open source product. This means anyone, anywhere in the world, can access the product's source code and step-by-step building guide for free. He also sells building kits on his website. Luis hopes that interested developers will access the open source code and help improve the eye board, making it more and more accessible to those who need it most. When asked about the future of his invention, Luis explained, "I would like to see the eye board used daily by people with disabilities that really need it to use the computer or communicate with others."

Luis is a native of La Ceiba, Honduras, a Caribbean port city 252 miles North of Tegucigalpa. Honduras is the second poorest country in Central America. Nearly 65% of its population lives in poverty and many more are underemployed. Luis grew up among classmates who lacked vision, encouragement, financial support or personal drive to pursue further education and improve their life circumstances.

Biography

At age 14, Luis began teaching himself electronics and computer programming languages. Instead of going outside to play soccer with friends, he would sit and read books. He dreamed of becoming a video game programmer. Luis recalls, "I started to create different projects for [my own] learning purposes, such as video games on the computer, and simple electronic circuits with digital interfaces." That same year, Luis created the first Honduran-built video game system (a video link and DIY info are available at intelseth.com).

When he was 17, Luis arranged to move to Colorado Springs, Colorado, USA, to finish high school. He hoped that this move would open doors for him that were not yet available in his home country. It was here in his senior year of high school that he met a classmate who was paraplegic (i.e. without use of his arms). Luis discovered how expensive it was for his classmate to use a computer. This experience motivated Luis to explore more cost-effective eye-tracking devices for his friend and others like him. It was October, 2010 when he began investigating how to improve a human-to-computer interface for people with disabilities. By March, 2011, Luis had a completed product—his eye board. In five short months he had channeled his digital video gaming skills into the creation of a valuable biomedical computer program (worn on a pair of glasses) for persons with disabilities. The program uses electrodes to detect what a person is looking at on the computer screen (e.g. letters of the alphabet) and then sends signals to the cursor to form words. Instead of clicking a mouse or typing on a keyboard, users need only the use of their eyes to make their selections on the screen. Computer communication for persons with disabilities, especially for paraplegic or quadriplegic persons, has never been easier, or cheaper!

Luis' selfless work and innovative genius on the eye board project earned him international accolades, including recognition as one of Youth Service America's 25 Most Influential Young People in the World. Luis has since been interviewed by news and media around the world including CNN, *Tech-Crunch*, *Make Magazine*, *Gizmag*, *POPSCI*, *The Huffington Post*, *Sparkfun Electronics*, *Diálogo*, and Reuters.

Today, Luis is a college student searching for a university scholarship to further his post-secondary training. He continues to refine many other inventions, including an optical heart rate monitor that uses infrared LED and light sensors, a Morse decoder that can interpret and translate sounds into words, a software program that converts Fahrenheit to Celsius, a computer-controlled lawn sprinkler, and his most recent focus—the Smartbike—a wearable device aimed to make exercising more enjoyable and less strenuous, especially for those needing physical therapy and rehabilitation from injuries.

In preparation for this publication, Luis asked me to include this comment: "One of my dreams is to change people's lives through technology and encourage young innovators through my work. I believe we can all contribute to this world through technology." Whenever Luis returns home to visit family he also makes visits to local schools to share his message about how important and rewarding it is to dream big and never give up. He hopes to one day open his own tech business in Honduras and hire local employees. It is his dream of making a difference for good in the world that drives him to keep working hard, says Luis. "I believe technology that's aimed to improve someone's life should be accessible all over the world."

Quick Links

- https://www.youtube.com/watch?v=b6nIiZgY4lw
- https://www.youtube.com/watch?v=zObidmxnj5Y
- http://www.thextraordinary.org/luis-fernando-cruz
- http://www.huffingtonpost.com/2014/10/21/youngest-tech-innovators-worldwide_n_5902114.html

- http://www.gizmag.com/luis-cruz-eyeboard-eye-tracking-computer-interface/20500/
- http://dialogo-americas.com/en_GB/articles/saii/features/main/2012/07/12/feature-02
- http://www.intelsath.com (Luis' personal website)
- http://www.myicv.com/lcruz (Luis' curriculum vitae)
- lcruz@intelsath.com (email Luis)
- https://twitter.com/intelsath (Luis on Twitter)

Laura Mooney, University of Calgary, Alberta, Canada

Interlude 1

Freedom
Shannon Patrick Garrett, Jr.

Freedom.

What is freedom? Freedom is a feeling
of pride. It's like you have been in
your room for a long time and you feel
isolated. Your mean babysitter tells you
not to go anywhere.

But...

You run outside and the breeze is in your
face, birds tweet and the sun shines, you
get this feeling of freedom.

YOU GOTTA BE A REBEL!!

Break the chains! Go outside and get this
feeling of... Freedom... and pride...

Proud to be free.

When you feel down or life is hard just
think of freedom and remember the joy you
feel. Maybe your life will be a better
life because you are proud and free.

Shannon Patrick Garrett, Jr. 12 years old, Norfolk, Virginia, USA

Chapter 5

Tavi Gevinson, US

Empowerment of Teenage Girls

Miranda Campbell

Teva is known for her work dedicated to the empowerment of teenage girls. Her website acts as safe space and forum for discussion among teen girls. As such, Gevinson raises the visibility of feminism amongst teenage girls in the 21ˢᵗ century. While teenage girls and their interests are sometimes not taken seriously or are seen as frivolous, flighty or commercial, Gevinson's work highlights the difficulty of being a teen girl, along with the complexity, contradictions, and richness of their lives.

Tavi Gevinson was born on April 26, 1996 in OakPark, Illinois. In 2008, she started a blog called *Style Rookie*, and in 2011, she started on online feminist magazine for teenage girls called *Rookie*. The magazine publishes articles three times a day predominantly written by women, as well as by the teen girls who read the site themselves. The content of the website has been anthologized: *Rookie Yearbook One* was published in 2012; *Rookie Yearbook Two* was published in 2013; and *Rookie Yearbook Three* was published in 2014.

Because she came to be known through her online presence, her work has reached teen girls across the world. The 21ˢᵗ century has seen the rise of what has become known as the "fourth wave" of feminism. The "first wave" of feminism took place during the 19ᵗʰ and early 20ᵗʰ century, and mostly focused on women's suffrage, or the right to vote. The "second wave" of feminism started in the 1960s, and focused on a range of women's issues, including reproductive rights and equality in the workplace and in family life. The "third wave" of feminism began in the 1990s, and is usually seen a response to the second wave's focus on white women. Third-wave feminism raises issues relevant to queer and non-white women, and tackles issues ranging from gender stereotypes to sex positivity. In the digital age of the 21st century, the term "fourth wave "emerged as a way to register a new era of feminist organizing that takes place online and uses digital tools. Gevinson's work can be seen as part of this fourth wave of feminism.

Amongst other influences, Gevinson references the importance of the "riot grrrl" movement of the 1990s, which began in Olympia, Washington, and spread throughout the world. In this movement, women noted the lack of presence of women in punk scenes and the music industry at large, and took a do-it-yourself approach to making music, zines, and feminist organizing.

Early Days

In 2008, at age 11, Tavi Gevinson started a blog about fashion called *Style Rookie*. She was inspired by a friend's older sister who had her own fashion website. On her blog, Gevinson published photographs of herself in creative and unusual outfits, and wrote personal and witty commentary about fashion—both about fashion designers and about clothes in everyday life. Soon, she was receiving 30,000 hits a day on her blog, and attracted the attention of the fashion world. She was invited as a guest to New York Fashion Week and Paris Fashion Week. After that, she was invited as a speaker at panels such as "The Future of Fashion Blogging" and the "Generation Next Forum," which examined Generation Y's consumer habits. She was guest stylist for a fashion spread in *BlackBook*, guest-hosted *Fashion Television*, and was the youngest writer to publish an article in *Harper's Bazaar*.

Rookie Magazine

Origins

In 2010, Tavi Gevinson was an invited speaker at the Toronto IdeaCity conference, which is a conference whose tagline is "the smartest people, the biggest ideas," where known people in a variety of fields present their ideas. Gevinson was invited to speak about the fashion industry, but chose the topic of the importance of *Sassy* magazine for teen girls in the 1990s. Gevinson commented that in its day, *Sassy* set itself apart from other teen girl magazines, which instructed girls to be what boys wanted, or what their parents wanted. Instead, as Gevinson highlighted, *Sassy* emphasized a positive message of girls being themselves. She felt this type of magazine was still needed, as girls of all stripes still feel alienated, like underdogs, and a "*Sassy* of today… [would] tell us that our opinions matter, to think for ourselves, and that we matter and we should be ourselves." She stated, "The most subversive thing a magazine could do today … would be being honest, and encouraging teen girls to be vocal." Gevinson identified the *Sassy* approach to fashion, pop culture, celebrity, relationships, politics, feminism, and community, as well as its friendly, relaxed, non-condescending writing style as useful components to carry into a contemporary project.

In 2011, Gevinson moved away from fashion as her main creative outlet, and wrote on *Style Rookie* that she was interested in mixing fashion with other genres, such as music and movies, to express herself. In that same year, at the age of 15, Gevinson started *Rookie*, an online magazine for teenage girls that she still edits, and features writing predominantly by women and teen girls. Gevinson initially partnered with Jane Pratt, an editor who had previously worked on magazines directed towards teen girls, such as *Sassy* and *Jane*, but Gevinson now retains sole ownership of *Rookie*. Gevinson has written that she felt there was a void in popular culture and a lack of magazines directed to teenage girls that treated them as intelligent beings.

Goals and Orientation

"Feminist" has sometimes been a taboo word, and Gevinson has commented on the negative stereotypes associated with this word. Gevinson has embraced the feminist label from early on to describe herself and her work. *Rookie* focuses on empowerment for girls. It creates a space for girls to express and explore their identities, and to share their opinions while connecting with one another. Rookie acknowledges that adolescence can be a difficult time in life, especially for girls, and promotes making the best of it. Though the website often tackles weighty and serious subject matters, a tone of underlying enthusiasm and positivity nonetheless infuses the website as a whole.

Gevinson has commented that women's magazines can create a stressful atmosphere around fashion for girls, but Rookie discusses personal style and fashion in a way that is devoted to fun, creativity, and self-expression rather than pleasing others, which connects to the overall emphasis of *Rookie* on self-esteem and individuality for girls. While an interest in traditionally feminine things, like fashion, has sometimes been seen as unintelligent or frivolous, *Rookie* promotes acceptance of girls' interests and pursuits, whatever they may be.

Subject Matter and Organization

Rookie features writing on a variety of topics that impact and interest teen girls, including music, sexuality, friendship, relationships, self-esteem, body acceptance, science, technology, fashion, writing, film, and television. While some of these topics, like fashion, might traditionally be associated with teen girl magazines, other features, like astronomy, video games, and building your own computer, push the traditional perceptions of what teen girls' interests are. Articles on *Rookie* may take on serious topics like sexual assault, or be devoted to fun, like how awesome glitter is. *Rookie* also features interviews with celebrities and other known individuals in their fields. Rather than celebrity worship, the emphasis of these interviews is often how someone has pursued and realized their creative project or unique interest, which might inspire girls to find and pursue their own passions.

Articles on *Rookie* are often written in the first person, and often use personal experience to explore broader issues. The writing style on *Rookie* is often frank, honest, fun, witty, and accessible. This writing takes its readers seriously and delivers a positive feminist message for a teen audience. Past article titles include "How to Not Care What Other People Think of You," "An Actually Useful Article About Dressing for a Party" and "Mod Eye Makeup in like Five Minutes." Each month of the online magazine is centered on a central theme. Past themes have included topics like beginning, secret, girl gang, home, transformation, power, freedom, and play. Acknowledging how keeping up with online forums can sometimes feel overwhelming, Gevinson decided that articles would be posted on *Rookie* at a few, youth-friendly times of the day: after school, after dinner, and before bed.

Gevinson has suggested that she feels there are public misconceptions about false divides among girls: that there are girls who are "art kids" or interested in art and culture, and girls who are "cheerleader" types, and who are interested in mainstream things. *Rookie* blurs these lines, and acknowledges that a common experience of adolescence across social categories means sometimes feeling like an outcast. Teenage girls are interested in a variety of topics, some niche, and some not. For example, *Rookie* features a "Friday Playlist" in its music category, and these playlists feature music from different genres and eras, some obscure, some not. One recurring feature of *Rookie* is the "Literally the Best Thing Ever" column, which celebrates the author's favorite thing, as particular or random as it may be: favorite musicians or films, authors, television shows, theme parks, *Keeping up with the Kardashians*, the mall, or open-source software, for example.

Rookie Community

One emphasis of *Rookie* is the idea of building an online community for girls: readers and writers of the *Rookie* site are called "rookies." Readers are invited to submit their writing, photos, videos, and comics to the site. The content of the *Rookie* website has also been published in three anthologies: *Rookie Yearbook One, Rookie Yearbook Two,* and *Rookie Yearbook Three,* in which Gevinson has edited together content from each year of the website's existence. Rookie has also hosted events for readers and contributors to meet one another. In 2012, Gevinson and her friend and *Rookie* magazine contributor, photographer Petra Collins, embarked on the "*Rookie* Road Trip," in which they travelled across American to 16 cities and hosted events attended by Rookie readers. In Los Angeles, an installation was created with teen girls bringing souvenirs from their bedrooms to the event, held at Space 15 Twenty.

TEDx Talk: "Still Figuring it Out"

In 2012, Gevinson delivered a TEDx Talk titled "Still Figuring it Out," in which she discussed the representation of strong women characters in the media. Giving the example of Catwoman, Gevinson argued that these women are often flat, as they have only one characteristic, such as sexuality, that is played up to suggest that the female character is strong. Gevinson counters that women—strong women—are complicated, multifaceted, and have flaws. She states this strong and nuanced portrayal of teenagers in particular is lacking in today's media landscape, and that intelligence and attractiveness, or feminism accompanied with an interest in fashion, are perceived as contradictory or irreconcilable factors in teen girls. *Rookie* aims to counter these notions, and Gevinson suggests that the website does not intend to portray a one-dimensional idea of empowerment for girls as being strong, being consistent, or having all the answers. Gevinson offers a different definition of feminism for teen girls, one that embraces contradictions and having different dimensions. She states the *Rookie* is not intended to give girls the answers while they are "still figuring it out" during their adolescence, but is intended to enable girls to find answers themselves.

Mobilizing the Rookie Community and Support for Malala

While much of *Rookie* is centered on inner self-discovery and acceptance, it also promotes engagement with the world and mobilizes teen girls. For example, ten days after Malala Yousafzai was shot in 2012, Gevinson organized an online Get Well card and letter drive for Yousafzai. *Rookie* readers from around the world sent in their thoughts, wishes, artwork, and poems for Yousafzai, which were posted on the *Rookie* site.

Support for Women's Rights

Gevinson has participated in other political actions connected to women's rights. In 2012, Gevinson participated in a public service announcement-style video campaign about women's health and reproductive rights, in support of Barack Obama's re-election. The video, which debuted on YouTube, was created by Sarah Sophie Flicker, a filmmaker and leader of New York's The Citizens Band, a group that uses cabaret and performance to make political statements. The video cites then-Republican candidate Mitt Romney's plans to overturn the *Roe v. Wade* legal decision, which made abortion legal in America, and to defund Planned Parenthood, an organization dedicated to women's reproductive health issues, as well as other policy moves contrary to women's interests. This video features a montage of a variety of young women, including Gevinson, lip synching to the Lesley Gore song, "You Don't Own Me." Gore opens the video by stating: "I recorded 'You Don't Own Me' in 1964 and it's hard for me to believe, but we're still fighting for the same things we were then. Yes, ladies, we've got to come together, get out there and vote, and protect our bodies. They're ours. Please vote."

Current Activities

Today, Tavi Gevinson continues to explore diverse creative outlets. While she is still the editor-in-chief of *Rookie* magazine, she no longer contributes many written pieces to the website. She has appeared on the television show *Parenthood*, and acted in the film *Enough Said*. In 2014, Tavi played the role of Jessica in a Broadway staging of the play *This is Our Youth*, written by Kenneth Lonergan. Gevinson has commented that a first reading or impression of Jessica as a character is that she is abrasive—a girl who argues, yells, and get mad, but a more thorough engagement with this character reveals much more to unpack, and her layers and complexity.

Gevinson graduated from high school in 2014. She is active in politics and acting. She has received many accolades and has been listed in several "best of" lists. She was selected for the *Forbes* 30 Under 30 in media list in 2011 and 2012. *The Huffington Post* included her in its 2012 18 "Under 18: HuffPost Teen's List Of The Most Amazing Young People Of The Year" list. In 2014, Gevinson was featured in *Time* magazine's "Most Influential Teens" list, noted for role as a teen in the internet age.

The empowerment of girls and young women takes many forms. Express yourself and participate in what interests you!

Quick Links

- To read or contribute to *Rookie* magazine, visit http://www.rookiemag.com/

- Many cities across the world now have Rock n' Roll Camps for Girls: feminist organizations dedicated to the empowerment of girls through music education. You might be interested in attending or volunteering at one of these camps. Visit the Girls Rock Camp Alliance website http://girlsrockcampalliance.org/ to see if there is a Rock Camp in your city; if not, start your own!

- To learn more and get involved in issues related to women's reproductive and sexual health, visit the Planned Parenthood website: http://www.plannedparenthood.org/

Miranda Campbell, Ryerson University, Toronto, Ontario, Canada

Chapter 6

Elba Hernandez, Guatemala

Let Girls Lead

Lara Forsberg

Elba Graciela Velasquez Hernandez, was born April 21, 1997, one year after the Guatemala peace accords were signed, bringing a formal end to one of the most brutal civil wars of the 20th century. Elba is from Conception Chiquirchapa, a beautiful small Maya Mam community in the western highlands of Guatemala; it is cooler there, than where large fruit plantations monopolize most of the fertile land. The town is surrounded by less valuable, small rural farms. People make a small living, often just enough to sustain them. For Elba the small plots of land they farm are a tapestry of farming autonomy and diversity. The Maya have traditionally worked for large fruit and coffee plantations and sixty five per cent of fertile land is owned by 2.1 per cent of the population. Elba knows that her future depends on her education, in Guatemala most rural women must work very hard never get a chance to earn a degree or finish a trade school.

Many Maya peasant women weave for extra income, and there is both cultural and economic significance to this. Backstrap loom weaving, an art, has been a distinctive part of the Maya culture, which was lost in colonization. Colours and designs have specific meanings and women say weaving the traditional huipiles makes them feel more a part of their culture and that they find solace in traditional weaving when overcoming the trauma of the civil war.

Elba is known for her weaving, she crafts beautiful multi-coloured designs; sold cheap on the Guatemala market. Her artwork is not quantified by the many hours of labour it takes to weave; she is not paid by the hour, she gets what people are willing to pay, this is simple capitalism, and the source of widespread unrest in Central America.

The Maya have been struggling for 20 years to get accords written in 1996, ending the civil war, to be implemented. Language barriers are still pervasive, the current telecommunications law does not allow for non-profit community radio, hospitals and doctors often require bribery and long distances to travel, and most infrastructure files need to be badly updated. Though Guatemala demands a high corporate tax, Otto Pérez Molina, The country's current president, and former military leader, is directly linked to Guatemala's violent past. The government needs people who understand policy, they need technicians to update files and reduce bureaucracy. Elba represents one of many of the new stewards of change in Guatemala. In 2013, Elba, and the girls of Let Girls Lead, transformed girl's lives and improved their community, ensuring that girls can go to schools. Elba is working to become a Judge someday; she has faith that Guatemala can achieve more political justice. Elba says that people are seeing the necessity of living under a system with political justice but that only then they we have a better life.

Maya people are a source of cheap labour for mostly American industry. Slavery lasted 500 years, increasing Spanish wealth. Slave labour in Guatemala spured the turn of phrase *banana republic* as the United Fruit Company made centuries of human rights violations advantageous for American industry. In the 1930's United Fruit provided some infrastructure in exchange for low taxes, but they owned most of the fertile land and had the protection of Guatemala's military junta to keep wages low. Low wages and unsafe work conditions, such as dusting of insecticides, killing people sometimes, among other work related injuries, lead to conflict. Unions were a threat to United Fruit, and other agro-industry elitists, and labour leaders were murdered by the government, with the help of CIA. Civil war between labour and government was inevitable. For girls like Elba, though the war is over, the psychological and economic effects of war and unchecked capitalism still linger.

Elba's grandfather observed a socialist movement during the Guatemalan Revolution from 1944–1955. In 1944, first president elected to serve the people, Juan Jose Arevalo, began his reforms to increase the minimum wage and re-distribute land. The Spiritual Socialist movement was made to look like a communist threat through American propaganda His reforms required landowners to provide schools, hospitals and homes for their poverty stricken workers whose labour provided the wealth of the land owners, the military and the Catholic Church. The Revolution was ended with an American covert operation known as PBSUCCESS, an undercover operation, carried out by the CIA that helped to depose of the democratically elected President Jacobo Arbendz. American interference increased the difficulties for the Maya people to make a decent wage, as well as students and other innovators to help them achieve equality and fairness under the law.

Elba's mother and father did not experience the freedom of the Spiritual Socialist movement, when students were granted freedom and autonomy in universities and Che Guevara fags flew unfettered. Unfortunately the memories of Elba's parents would be marked by the government reprisals upon students and union leaders as well as the mass genocide of Mayas in the 80's. Whole Maya villages were destroyed in the 'scorched earth' campaign in the highlands. Maya's and activists were jailed and approximately 100,000 were murdered or assassinated. 46,000 people disappeared when they stood in opposition to the United Fruit monopoly, and other slave labour proponents. One million were displaced by the political violence. These displaced have no papers to show they are citizens of Guatemala and cannot take advantage of social programs such as health care that help to strengthen Guatemala.

30,000 people were made to disappear. People reported helicopters, that would pick up people and drop them in the ocean, or bury them in mass graves (Lillian, 2015). Maya people give personal testimony to acts of torture. Peasant men having their ears cut off, their finger nails removed and then burned alive while peasants were forced to watch. The Catholic Church at this time aligned with the military. Government soldiers preyed on unprotected women, forcing their obedience through psychological warfare, disappearances of their children as well as rape and other dehumanizing forms of victimization.

Violence against women is widespread in Guatemala. It is a difficult endeavour that provides little justice when Police, lawyers and judges, who often accept bribes and exploit women themselves, hold the positions of power. Police and military involvement, in serious crimes such as kidnapping, drug trafficking, and extortion, (htt4) make laying charges for women difficult.

Against this, the backdrop women have fear for their own safety as well as the safety of their children, and this cycle will continue to prevent necessary social movements to succeed. For people to advocate for themselves, this pattern of domination will need to be replaced without consistent role models, protectors and fathers to help them. Many Maya men experience unemployment, alcoholism, child abandonment and family violence, a cycle that has put everyone at a disadvantage. Today people are still being kidnapped and burned alive, resulting from drug wars and family rivalries, atrocities have become the norm, and this violence perpetuates the gender gap. Elba says that just by going to school, she has "changed the perceptions of her parents." Elba feels that "The Community has begun to see the necessities of boys, girls and adolescents and to seek for their protection."

Elba helps with her five younger brothers and sisters and she faces discrimination hindering her education. Elba says that girls are not supported to stay in school, and that her parents wanted to pull her out of school because they didn't think it was important to invest so much in a daughter who would likely end up a housewife.

Catholic Canon law teaches that girls should be ready for marriage by the age of 14 and in Guatemala; the legal age of marriage is 14 with parental consent. The Catholic Church also opposes birth control resulting in early pregnancy and child marriage. Deadly complications for both mother and child result in adolescent pregnancy. Rural girls, like Elba, are not close to a hospital when predictable complications result from adolescent pregnancy. Death is a common outcome for vulnerable mothers both mother and fetus. When birth control is not introduced to an adolescent, she is naïve about her own body and the lifelong dedication motherhood requires; pregnancy can end hopes for an education and a living wage. Girls must withdraw from their educations and are subject to physical and sexual violence when they are young and inexperienced and do not know their rights.

Elba noted, "The lack of educational opportunities and the discrimination against Maya girls and women are the biggest barriers facing girls like me. I desperately wanted to continue my studies because I liked participating in class and dreamed of one day becoming a lawyer. My grandfather (who had witnessed the Spiritual Socialism that enabled universities to thrive) had always encouraged me to stay in school and he was able to help me convince my parents that I deserved an education just as much as my brothers. These experiences made me realize that I needed to stand up and speak on behalf of other girls."

Like different colours of wool on a loom, building a country takes many people, men and women, supporting one another. Elba found a strong ally in her teacher Professor Jose Lopez who introduced her to the Let Girls Lead program; there she met Juany Garcia, who helped the girls develop these plans to bring their concerns to the community. With regular leadership meeting, girls began to take pride in themselves, Elba says that "through these programs we began to learn the capacity that we as people possess and that there is no reason or difference between men and women.

These opportunities led to Elba starring in the film ¡PODER!, about her life, and that of her friend Emelin. In ¡PODER! the girls speak for themselves, much as they are doing in their communities. The award winning film highlighted cultural obstacles. In the film, Elba goes through a process of trying to get girls to be "consulted on issues that matter with representation, when advocating for themselves." Elba hopes for girls everywhere to be able to enjoy their rights with dignity; these include the right to education, health, protection, and participation.

"When I was 12 years old, we visited the Mayor of Chiquirchapa, along with our peers and the Mayor told us that he could not attend to us because he had something important to address. On our Second visit, he told us that we should come back another day because he was busy, and on the third time we visited him, he met with us." With a positive attitude and determination Elba gained the support of the Mayor, as well as religious and community leaders. Elba's success can be partially attributed to her clever approach in engaging the Mayor's interest. It was Juany Garcia's idea to appeal to his fatherly sentiments. The girls correctly pointed out that their goal was to build a better community for all girls, including his own daughter. So when the Mayor opened the door to them and they explained their obstacles regarding their health education and future, he agreed to listen to them.

The girls were given the task of researching the needs of the adolescent girls in the community and to assist in implementing them personally with the mayor. This was both an honor and a huge responsibility.Elba did the research and she engaged local leaders to support her. She gives thanks to the support of Professor José López and Lincenciada Juany García Pérez, and they attained program funding to support girls' education, health and safety in her community in 2013, Elba and the girls of *Let Girls Lead* assisted in the process.

The rights and the livelihoods of children had already been written into the constitution in 1996, but the people must speak; "one voice one vote," says Elba. Elba says that she and the girls at *Let Girls Lead* have learned about advocacy and human rights, practiced [their] public speaking skills, and developed a policy proposal to fund girls' education and health programs in [their] community. It took some convincing, but the Mayor finally agreed to fund our proposal, and is now one of our biggest supporters. We achieved this milestone in a town where fewer than 10% of girls complete school, which is a major achievement. People have started to take notice of our success, and with the help of *Let Girls Lead* and Emmy-winning filmmaker Lisa Russell, we're sharing our story in ¡PODER!, our short film. "I hope that girls in other countries see ¡PODER! and are inspired to create change in their communities too," (http://www.letgirlslead.org/poder).

By partnering with other organizations and using existing legislations, such as the 1996 Peace Accords, the United Nations Convention on the Rights of the Child and the UN Declaration on the Rights of Indigenous Peoples, Elba and people like her will hold the Guatemala's government responsible. Using already established international charters, the weaker smaller threads, of children and adolescent girls, can be re-enforced with the help of strong adults. Elba's tenacity in consulting the constitution on the rights and livelihoods of children helped them open a community center that would focus on girl's education. They allocated funding of, 0.5% of the town budget to open a Municipal Office of Childhood and Adolescence, as well as two million quetzals ($250,000). This team of girls, supporting one another through the *Let Girls Lead* program has developed policy to help girls to reduce gender based violence, to support girls to finish school, to see a doctor when they needed and to engage in civil change and advanced education. *Let Girls Lead* has been of global service. " The Future of 2030 Depends on our decision to invest in adolescent girls," says Elba.

Quick Links

- http://www.c-r.org/accord-article/guatemala%E2%80%99s-peace-process-context-analysis-and-evaluation
- http://www.ticotimes.net/2015/02/16/guatemalas-indigenous-peoples-change-strategy-to-seek-more-political-representation
- http://www.cnn.com/2014/04/10/world/un-world-murder-rates/
- http://www.osac.gov/pages/ContentReportDetails.aspx?cid=15656
- http://www.forbes.com/sites/deniserestauri/2013/10/09/a-teen-girls-secret-to-finding-real-power-fix-something-thats-broken/
- http://www.letgirlslead.org/poder
- http://reports.weforum.org/global-gender-gap-report-2014/
- Interview: Lillian. Nobleford, Alberta: January 2015. http://culturalsurvival.org/news/recognizing-women-leaders-community-radio-stations-guatemala

Lara Forsberg, Writer, Nobleford, Alberta, Canada

Chapter 7

Celia Ho, China

The Elephant Girl

Tanya Merriman

Celia Ho, a young student from Hong Kong, China, is known around the world as "The Elephant Girl." Shocked by the horror of ivory trade, Celia wrote to her local newspaper addressing her concerns. To raise awareness, she created a poster and used it to plead for elephant protection around the world.

Celia was born in China at the very beginning of the 21st century. As a student in Hong Kong, Celia wasn't an activist until she was deeply moved by an article she read about the brutality and senselessness of elephant poaching in the magazine called *National Geographic*. As the place of an emerging wealthy class that is the result of new business and massive economic growth, China is the world's leading consumer of ivory, or the material that comes from elephant tusks. Once reserved for the aristocracy and the ruling class, ivory has tremendous artistic and cultural significance. Because of its beauty, rarity and durability, ivory has been a sought after symbol of status throughout history. China's new elite has created an unprecedented desire for ivory with a high cost that is putting the entire elephant species at risk. Sadly, many consumers hold the false belief that the ivory that they purchase comes from elephants that have died a natural death, Celia has made it her mission to educate consumers both locally and globally, and to recruit the young people of her own generation completely stop the demand for ivory so that the poaching ends with them.

Celia Ho is a very young woman fighting some very old mindsets and beliefs. Known as the around the world as the Elephant Girl, Celia is fighting a tough fight against elephant poaching and the consumption of ivory for decorative and medicinal purposes. Every year, the number of elephants poached, or hunted and killed illegally, around the world for their tusks is well into the hundreds of thousands. The tusks are forcibly removed and then used, as a material known as ivory, to create sculptures, jewelry, and chopsticks or to be ground into a powder and used for medicinal purposes. The tusks are actually large incisor teeth that occur in the male and female of the species. The tusks do not grow back and the vast majority of tusks that are sold through the ivory trade come from animals that are savagely killed—not from those that perished from natural causes, which is a largely held misconception. Generally, the male elephants are killed for the tusks, but because elephants are communal and will be found in their environment together, the females and babies are usually killed in process as well. The tusks are very valuable and, therefore, the elephant population is very vulnerable. In fact, *National Geographic* asserts the numbers may be as high as between 30,000 and 38,000 elephants in Africa alone slaughtered for their tusks.

Elephants are the largest animals in Earth and amongst the smartest and gentlest too. They are beautiful, majestic animals that are also very empathic and sensitive to their world and to one another. Living in large, social groups called herds; elephants are very communal and even share childcare duties and appoint other elephants in their herd to babysit! Their community is very important to their welfare and they even say hello and welcome one another after extended absence with an intense and happy elephant song and dance called a greeting ceremony. They take care of one another when they are sick, and they hug one another too. And it is true that elephants never forget. Elephants cry; they mourn when another member of their herd family dies, and they recognize one another jubilantly, even after years or decades of separation. Elephant babies are completely dependent on the mothers for the first three years of life, and they continue to stay with their families until they are around sixteen years-old. Elephant mothers, called matriarchs, fight fiercely to protect their babies when they are in danger, and this is perhaps the most heartbreaking part of elephant poaching: Many of the elephants die trying to protect their young from the horrible attacks.

And, elephant poaching is incredibly horrible. The horror and brutality of elephant poaching might be too much for some people to manage, but not Celia Ho. She has fought her battle against poaching despite the appalling and painful realities and the deeply held mindsets she must confront as she fights.

Elephant poaching is the most prevalent in areas of the African continent where poverty is the highest. In Coastal East Africa, the countries of Kenya, Tanzania, Mozambique and Zimbabwe have the richest elephant populations but also face the toughest challenges of recovering from colonial rule and resource exploitation. Centuries of this shattering destruction have left these countries with crippling poverty and few ways to build income. Entire communities of people are desperate for basic necessities like food to eat and a safe place to sleep; in this context, it is somewhat understandable that someone would go to extremes to obtain an ivory tusk, which could bring in hundreds of thousands of dollars. The illegal poaching business in Africa, estimated in the billions, is grim, yet profitable. Simultaneously, in Asian countries such as China and Vietnam, a rising middle class searches for ways to demonstrate new wealth and status. They enjoy purchasing ivory, once only available to wealthiest business leaders and the aristocracy, because of its beauty and symbolism. These same countries value the long held beliefs about religious beliefs, artistic expression and medicine, so ivory has other significance and use as well. In combination, these two circumstances create a huge, profitable and devastating demand of and supply for ivory that is threatening to erase the entire elephant population from the world.

The act of poaching elephants is nothing short of horrific. There is no humane way to extract the large tusks from the elephants. The animals are not anesthetized or protected from pain. Instead, the elephants are shot with heavy ammunition or trapped in wire snares that shred their feet. Even if they are not the targets, the females are usually trapped and killed as well, or worse they will die trying to protect the elephant babies. The final act of brutality it to use an axe to remove the face of the elephant in order to remove the tusks.

The fight to end elephant poaching is not just the sentimental hope of one young girl. While poaching does bring enormous profit to the poachers and traders, the short and long term cost of this grisly industry is high and, perhaps, irreversible. If poaching of elephants continue at the same rate as the last decades, elephants will become extinct. The Coastal East African countries are already experience dramatic loss of elephant populations. For example, twenty years ago, Chad had elephant numbers upwards of 40,000. Now, the number of elephants is closer to 2000. Overall, the entire population of elephants as decreased from over 10 million to less than one half a million in total. The loss of lives is not just to elephants. Hundreds of humans have died throughout the years as a result of the ivory trade. They die as a result of getting caught in the violence of the poaching operations or they die trying to protect the elephants from harm. As the poaching of ivory becomes more and more technologically advanced and sophisticated, the danger and risk will increase as well. It is likely that more people involved in these operations will die before the poaching comes to an end altogether. Continued loss of human life and the threat of extinction to elephants are both significant problems.

Elephants are known as a keystone species. This means that they are species whose presence is necessary to the health and survival of the ecosystem in which it lives. This means that if we lose our elephants we will stand to lose an important part of the planet, and all of the other plant and animals that depend on this part of the planet, as well. This is a very disturbing possibility. Because of the urgency and gravity of the situation, many people with even higher profiles than Celia have joined this fight, too. Internationally known basketball player Yao Ming, known for being a Houston Rocket and the tallest person in the NBA, has taken many trips to places like Kenya to see these placid and intelligent creatures. He is working with organizations like Wild Aid to increase awareness and change peoples' thinking; including the common belief that ivory comes from elephants that have dies from natural causes. Similarly, actress Li Bingbing, known for her action-packed work in the *Resident Evil* movies, acting as a United Nations Environment Programme (UNEP) Goodwill Ambassador, has worked extremely hard to change thinking. This includes making a video, just like Celia did, to highlight the magnificence of the elephants and the horror of the poaching industry. Even world famous actor and all around cultural icon Jackie Chan is working as an ambassador to raise awareness and change attitudes in his home country of China, which is the largest market for illegal ivory.

Like many young activists who are working hard to change the world, Celia Ho is not especially wealthy, she is not world famous or even especially tall—Celia became an activist because her heart was broken. Thankfully, she did not witness any particular atrocity and survive any particular conflict. She was not beckoned or even asked. Celia was called into action only because she was incredibly troubled by something she read. After reading an article in *National Geographic* called "Blood Ivory" that explained and illustrated the horrors of the ivory trade, the threat to the elephant species, and the role that Chinese consumers play in sustaining the ivory trade, she became determined that she would take any risk and use every opportunity to use her voice to change peoples' minds about ivory. And, like many young activists who are working hard to change the world, she also decided to take her anger and sorrow and channel it into working hard. It has become her mission to convince people that selling of ivory and the slaughter of elephants would end with her generation.

Celia knew that she had a big challenge ahead of her. The first important thing she realized was that her own country of China was deeply complicit as the primary consumers of ivory. Ivory is made into jewelry and everyday decorative items, and Celia saw clearly that these smart, gentle creatures should not have to endure brutalization and suffering only to create trinkets. Realizing that she would have to convince people that this fight mattered and that, while the buying and selling of ivory may not connect to their daily lives, they should increase their own awareness, share the message with others, and most importantly, make the right decision should they find themselves in a position to purchase ivory jewelry or household decorations themselves.

One doesn't need to organize a rally thousands of people to be an effective and inspiring activist. In fact, Celia Ho's activism has taken many unique and effective forms. Each of her efforts plays a small part to reach, inform and motivate people to refuse to buy or use decorative ivory. This will change minds and save the lives of countless elephants as a result. Her small but strong operation has three major objectives: To educate her country with correct and relevant information about the ivory trade; to attract international attention to the campaign against ivory traffic; to mobilize young people to take responsibility for making the fight against ivory their own and to make sure that the trade of ivory ends with them.

The first of her many steps started with a letter to her local newspaper, *The South China Morning Post*. Celia's letter was so impressive that she immediately gained attention and support from her community. Next, she organized social media and letter writing campaigns that focused on educating schools and parents about the terrible ivory trade. Celia uses social media as a tool for organizing people and sharing information. Her sites are interesting, informative and relevant. Her social media efforts also help to grow and connect her community. Her fans can share their own ideas and encouragement with Celia and with one another using the comments features on each of her sites. From here she began to unite a passionate community of protesters and at this point something even more amazing began to happen: Celia created a community of people who shared her vision, and her community's support and enthusiasm for her started to motivate her to do even more and work even harder. At this point she needed to more tools do the work, so she created her widely known educational poster with the title, Don't Buy Ivory, and she created her own website from which the poster can be downloaded. Celia even participated in a fashion campaign that informs people about the horrors of the ivory trade with t-shirts that have catchy slogans about protecting elephants. She has created several short videos in 2013; Celia created what might be her most passionate and interesting kind of unique activism: She wrote a song called "This Ache," about mother elephants and their babies that are set to a melody originally written by the very popular Lana Del Rey. This is a very personal and sensitive contribution—it demonstrates how deeply she cares about the work she is doing. It is also very inspiring, and the response she received from this song and video clearly shows that she is reaching people and making them care as much as she does. The song's beautifully haunting and sad lyrics have moved even more people to become informed about the tragic and horrible ivory industry.

All of these efforts demonstrate what could be the most important outcome of Celia's work. The tools we need to become an activist are already in our hands. She has done everything armed with only information, her own voice, her creativity and her own passion. her knowledge and information will make a difference to the elephants that she so fiercely defends. The brutal slaughter of elephants and their babies can come to an end with one generation. And the best news is that once the elephants are left with peace and safety it won't take long for their population to increase and for their entire species to be restored to their rightful and wonderful place. Celia's work has made a difference.

Celia's passion and hard work will guarantee life and safety for elephants of yours and future generations. This is her contribution. But, Celia also shows us that anyone who feels strongly about a cause and chooses to translate this strength into action can make a difference. She shows us that everyone has his or her own power; this, too, is a contribution that matters.

Quick Links

- https://www.youtube.com/watch?v=78Amr8j9y90#t=249
- http://news.nationalgeographic.com/news/2014/06/140616-elephants-tusker-satao-poachers-killed-animals-africa-science/

Tanya Merriman, University of Southern California

Interlude 2

Uncertainty
Sarah Thirkell

my entire life,
i've had this desire
to achieve something great

instead,
i am often troubled
by the inevitable fate
of being average

average amounts
to virtually nothing
i refuse to lack the courage
of being something
unique

someone
someone with
their soul on fire
awaiting
higher destinations

i've thought
long and hard
inorder to uncover
how i can compel
a change in this
world

yet my mind
is clouded
with infestations
of unanswered questions

perpetually
i am left
with the same
senseless condition:
uncertainty

somehow
beyond all doubt
i've found peace
with the knowledge
that acceptance
trumps all
the unknown

acceptance amounts
to anything and everything
i choose to allow
myself
to be me

acceptance
grants you
the liberation
to a life free
from dread and worry
as you realize
that not everything
can be explained
and instead
appreciated for
their self-contained
mystery

perhaps
this is not
the truth you seek
but why delay the day
when you will
end worrying
and commence
existing

Sarah Thirkell, Grade 10, William Aberhart High School, Calgary, Alberta, Canada

Sarah's channel, video of poem: https://youtu.be/yMeIC6tBG5Q

Chapter 8

Natividad Llanquileo, Chile

Speaking for Indigenous Political Prisoners

Fernanda Soler-Urzúa & Michelle Harazny

Natividad Llanquileo is a fierce Indigenous rights activist in Chile. At the age of 24, she became the chosen spokesperson of Mapuche political prisoners. Her activist efforts have focused on fighting the criminalization of the struggles of the Mapuche people and the militarization of their territories.

Issues of Land Rights Facing the Mapuche People in Chile

According to Bengoa (1996), there is ample evidence that the Mapuche people have been living in their territories since approximately 600 B.C.E. He asserts that before Spaniards came, the Mapuche people had some contact with the Inca from the north, who made it to the central part of Chile by the end of the 15th century. When the first contacts with Spaniards were made in the 16th century, Mapuche people inhabited the vast majority of the southern territory of Chile (Comisión de Verdad Histórica y Nuevo Trato con los Pueblos Indígenas, 2003).

The Spanish quickly started to seize Mapuche land, and they had occupied the vast majority of it between 1598 and 1604 (Comisión de Verdad Histórica y Nuevo Trato con los Pueblos Indígenas, 2003). The area called Pikunmapu was seized by the Spaniards, together with Chiloé Island, which was part of Willimapu. However, the Mapuche managed to keep control of their land that reaches from the south of the Bío-Bío River (in what is now known as the Bío Bío Region) to the border of the Butalmapu and Gullumapu, except for Chiloé Island—located in what is now known as the Lakes Region. It took Spaniards, and later Chileans, more than 260 years to seize this Mapuche land after several failed attempts (Bengoa, 1996).

After the creation of the Chilean Republic in 1810, Mapuche people still resisted the occupation of their territories. Desperate to use the natural resources from this region for economic expansion, the newly formed Chilean state started a campaign to urbanize and occupy Mapuche land in order to exploit it. In 1881, the Mapuche found themselves outnumbered and were unable to stop the occupation of their territories. Since then, they have been constantly harassed to cede their lands (Comisión de Verdad Histórica y Nuevo Trato con los Pueblos Indígenas, 2003). The attempts by the state to assimilate the Mapuche population into mainstream Chilean society have been constant, and still continue to the present day.

"As long as there is a community threatened by repression, as long as there is a Mapuche child attacked, as long as there is a Mapuche community member detained, killed or tortured, I will be there, raising my voice and denouncing the atrocities along with my people, demanding what sustains our lives, which is the liberation of our people," Natividad notes.

Natividad Llanquileo was born on the Esteban Yevilao Mapuche reserve in Puerto Choque, Bío Bío, Chile on July 14, 1984 (Correa Agurto, 2014; Llanquileo, 2009). She comes from a family of activists. Her father, Juan Llanquileo, was an active member in their community and participated in land reclamation actions during Salvador Allende's government. Juan was detained on several occasions and was forced to go into hiding because of the risk of political persecution (Correa Agurto, 2014). He passed away in 2007.

Natividad's family currently owns around 50 acres of land and grows beans, potatoes and wheat. Her family's land is now worn out due to environmental overuse, causing her family to live in poverty (Llanquileo, 2009). Natividad enjoyed spending time at the lake on her reserve and looking at the intense green color of the trees since she was young. She defines her land and the reserve as an oasis. Unfortunately, her oasis is now being exploited by the forestry companies Volterra and Mininco (Correa Agurto, 2014).

Natividad attended a school located close to home. However, when she was 14 years-old, she was forced to leave her reserve to finish high school at a boarding school in Los Álamos, Bío Bío (Correa Agurto, 2014). For the following five years, she returned home every weekend to spend time with her family. When Natividad finished high school, she tried to find a job in the nearby towns, but was unsuccessful. She knew she needed to work in order to pay for university, so she decided to move to Santiago when she was 19.

Natividad knew nothing about Santiago except that it was a very large city (Correa Agurto, 2014). She was surprised to find out how large a city it was. Once in Santiago, she contacted a job agency that was looking for "girls from the south." In the Chilean context, "girls from the south," *o niñas del sur,* usually means rural, Indigenous, young women who work as live-in nannies.

A very wealthy family hired Natividad to take care of the cleaning, the laundry, the cooking, and the babysitting. "It's one of the worst memories I have," she recalls (Correa Agurto, 2014, p. 95). She knew what time she had to wake up, but not what time she would go to bed. Natividad couldn't stand the working conditions for long, and she decided to return to her reserve.

A year later, when she was twenty, she decided to return to Santiago to work and attend law school. She had a full-time job as a nanny while she attended school in the evenings. When asked why she decided to go to law school, she said, "It was my attempt to find justice within injustice" (Totoro & Retamal, 2011). In 2007, Natividad's father passed away, and she decided to put a hold on her studies to spend time with her family. She went back to law school the following year.

Natividad and her brothers Ramón and Víctor Llanquileo have been active in the fight against land grabs by multinational forestry companies and the Chilean state. Both Ramón and Víctor were prosecuted for allegedly assaulting a public prosecutor. In 2010, after spending two years in custody awaiting a trial, Víctor was acquitted and Ramón was sentenced to fifteen years in prison for allegedly participating in the above-mentioned assault (Mapuexpress, 2011). This sentence was later reduced to eight years by the Supreme Court of Chile.

The trial Ramón and Víctor faced along with fifteen other Mapuche weichafe (warriors) has been highly questioned by both national and international human rights organizations, such as Observatorio Ciudadano and the Inter-American Court of Human Rights, which recently determined that the Chilean state had failed to grant due process in trials against Mapuche activists. The principle of double jeopardy was violated in this case, since these Mapuche weichafe were tried twice for the same offence, once by the state-run justice system and once in military proceedings.

Natividad was in her third year in law school in Santiago in 2010 when her brother and other Mapuche weichafe were taken to prison. While visiting her brother at a detention center in Concepción (the capital city of the Bío Bío region), Natividad was asked by Ramón and a group of Mapuche political prisoners to be their spokesperson and participate in actions against the persecution of her people.

As a law student, Natividad was very familiar with the judicial process and all its irregularities, and had a deep understanding of legal terms. She was able to speak to the press and put forth the demands of the prisoners who had by then started a hunger strike. Without much hesitation, she accepted the prisoners' petition, and started to meet with supporters to organize rallies and protests to bring the Mapuche demands to the public sphere.

Defending Mapuche Political Prisoners

It is impossible to understand Natividad's role in the fight for her people's rights without knowing what led her to become active in this struggle. What follows is an account of her involvement with Mapuche political prisoners.

In October 2008, an alleged assault on a public prosecutor in Puerto Choque took place. Natividad's brothers Víctor and Ramón, along with fifteen other Mapuche weichafe were accused of premeditated ambush and attempting to kill a public prosecutor named Elgueta. They were jailed over the course of the investigation, which took two years.

What was clear from the hearings was that there actually was a confrontation between police forces and Mapuche weichafe, who blocked a dirt road when they saw a police convoy going into their ancestral land, which was and is owned by the forestry companies Volterra and Mininco. Public prosecutor Elgueta was travelling with the police convoy, which the weichafe did not know, according to their own testimonies (Totoro & Retamal, 2011). Police forces attacked the weichafe when they found the blocked road, and attempted to kill them by shooting them at point blank range. (For firsthand accounts, please refer to Totoro and Retamal.)

Fully aware of the legal setup prepared by the public prosecutor's office to make a case against the weichafe and aware of the consequences they would face if they were found guilty during the trial that would start in November 2010, they decided to mobilize and organize a hunger strike in July 2018 across the different jails in which they were detained. Consequences for Natividad's brother Víctor and his friend Héctor Llaitul would be far-reaching, since they were accused of being the leaders of a Mapuche terrorist organization by the public prosecutor's office.

Speaking against the Justice System

The hunger strike was one of most massive mobilizations in recent Chilean history. Initially, 14 weichafe in the Concepción detention center started the hunger strike, along with another eight weichafe in the Temuco detention center. Over the following days, other weichafe in the jails of the Chilean south joined. Sixteen days after the strike had started, 34 Mapuche political prisoners had joined.

The jailed weichafe demanded to be tried in the ordinary justice system and not the military system, and that they not be charged under antiterrorism laws. They also demanded that the government release all Mapuche political prisoners from jail and demilitarize Mapuche land.

When the strike had been going on for 19 days, Natividad became the chosen spokesperson of the Mapuche political prisoners detained in the Concepción detention center. She had travelled all the way from Santiago to visit her family and jailed brothers, as she regularly did. When visiting her brother Víctor, she was asked by him and Héctor Llaitul to take on the role of spokesperson for them. Without much hesitation, and given the urgency of the current circumstances, she accepted.

Natividad defines herself as an introverted and rather shy woman. In fact, she says she did not enjoy presenting in front of her class when she was at school. However, she forgot about her stage fright and did not hesitate at all when she had to talk to the mainstream TV stations and radio broadcasters.

As the spokesperson of the weichafe in Concepción, she had to participate in several meetings with state officials to put forth their demands. Being in law school helped her a great deal in understanding all the legal irregularities of the investigation against her brothers and the rest of the weichafe.

Natividad was vocal in criticizing the Chilean government led by the right wing president Sebastián Piñera for not having referred publicly to the hunger strike during its first month. She also criticized the government for speaking about the Mapuche political prisoners as criminals who committed common crimes, which ignored the legitimate nature of their demand for self-determination, or the right to determine their own form of government and political status.

As Natividad had taken on the challenge to be the spokesperson of the Mapuche prisoners, she decided she would take a second leave from law school to support her people, and she would not return until her job was finished.

Reactions to the Hunger Strike

Mainstream media took its time to inform the public about the strike. The Chilean Order of Journalists denounced mainstream media for not reporting on the issue and demanded that they inform the general population of such important news.

Natividad and the other spokespeople for other weichafe worked hard to make the strike come to light by contacting alternative newspapers, online

TV channels and international media. It was this pressure, and the denouncement of the Order of Journalists that pushed mainstream media to report on the strike and the situation of the weichafe. Mainstream media followed their right-wing editorial policies, which portrayed the weichafe as savages and criminals.

Relatives, friends and spokespeople of the Mapuche prisoners, along with non-Mapuche allies organized protests in Santiago, Concepción and Temuco. These protests continued until the hunger strike was over, which lasted 81 days. Riot police fought the protesters with brutal violence and were constantly denounced by Natividad and other spokespeople in the alternative media. At times, there were more riot police officers than protesters. Frequently, protesters were indiscriminately battered before they could even start marching.

Around a month after the strike had started, government officials said that they would not intervene in a trial that was undertaken by the judiciary system, since it was the commitment of the government to respect court decisions, and said they would not take a stance regarding the trial. Instead, they filed a plea in court to forcibly feed the weichafe on strike, violating their right to undertake a legitimate strike. The weichafe categorically refused to be fed.

After 59 days of the hunger strike had passed, the Mapuche prisoners were in very poor health. It was then that opposition members of parliament (MPs) committed to drive a reform to antiterrorist laws. One of the opposition leaders called on the government to initiate dialogue with the Mapuche weichafe and their spokespeople.

The next day, the minister of the interior, Rodrigo Hinzpeter, finally announced that the government would present two bills to congress, one that would limit the jurisdiction of military justice and another that would introduce a reform to the antiterrorist laws. This initiative represented a success for the Mapuche. Even though military justice was not completely eliminated, the proposed bill would limit its power to prosecute Mapuche weichafe fighting for self-determination. By then, the government refused to participate in any dialogue with the weichafe. Since not all the Mapuche demands were being met, the political prisoners decided to continue with the strike.

When the strike had already been going on for two months, some opposition MPs joined the hunger strike in solidarity with the imprisoned weichafe. Workers from the National Workers Union and the Student Federation of Universidad de Chile soon followed.

Negotiating with the Government

The relatives and spokespeople of the weichafe, along with allies, started radicalizing their pressure tactics and organizing occupations of different significant places in Chile. One of the highlights was the occupation of the offices of the International Labour Organization in Santiago. Another one was the occupation of an important TV station by university students.

At day 74 of the strike, and when some of the prisoners had lost more than 30 pounds, the government established a dialogue with the spokespeople from the Mapuche, which was facilitated by priests from the Catholic Church. Mapuche spokespeople acknowledged that starting a dialogue was a step forward, but announced that the strike would continue.

Government officials were very hesitant about negotiating with the Mapuche prisoners, but at day 80 of the strike, the minister of the interior announced they would visit the weichafe on strike.

On day 81 of the strike, government officials met with Natividad and all other spokespeople. The government had brought a proposal that addressed all the demands of the weichafe. They made a commitment to carry out every task in their proposal through concrete actions. After nearly three months of hunger strike, and with several weichafe in the hospital for their poor physical condition, the hunger strike came to an end.

A month after the strike had ended, the hearings in court for the case of the alleged assault on public prosecutor Elgueta started. However, the office of the public prosecutor and the government persisted in pressing charges under the antiterrorism laws in this case, which clearly violated the agreement reached the previous month. Natividad called on international observers from different international organizations to come to Concepción to monitor the trial against the Mapuche weichafe.

Eleven weichafe, among which was Natividad's brother Víctor, were acquitted. However, her brother Ramón and three other Mapuche were sentenced to prison. The defense of the weichafe appealed the decision in the Court of Appeals, which refused their plea. Later on, the Supreme Court reduced their sentences, but did not rule out the use of antiterrorism laws. Natividad declared that it was unacceptable that the Supreme Court had legitimated the use of antiterrorism laws against Mapuche weichafe fighting for their rights.

Where is Natividad Now?

At the end of 2011, and after having done a great deal of work for a year and a half to put Mapuche demands on the table, Natividad decided that it was time to continue with law school. On her website, she wrote a public statement where she condemned the Chilean state and the justice system for having failed Indigenous peoples once more (Llanquileo, 2009). She also wrote:

> I have to say that my work defending the just cause of our people is not over and it will not stop. I will support, to the best of my abilities, all the fights of my people, in every reserve, in each land reclamation, and I will keep on demanding the abolition of antiterrorism laws and the releasing of all our political prisoners. I will be there, raising my voice and participating in every mobilization I learn about.

Natividad's goal is to become a lawyer, to put into practice what she first set as her main goal: to find justice within injustice.

Quick Links

Links related to Natividad's story (Chile):

- Natividad Llanquileo's blog during her time as spokesperson (in Spanish)
  http://natividadllanquileo.blogspot.com

- Natividad Llanquileo's Facebook page
  https://www.facebook.com/natividad.delc.3?fref=ts

- Observatorio Ciudadano (in Spanish)
  http://www.observatorio.cl/

Links to Indigenous Activist websites (Canada):

- Comité D'appui au peuple Mapuche (in Spanish)
  http://mapuchemontreal.wordpress.com/

- Women's coordinating committee for a free Walmapu
  http://wccctoronto.wordpress.com/

- Idle No More
  http://www.idlenomore.ca/

- Defenders of the Land
  http://www.defendersoftheland.org/

References

Bengoa, J. (1996). Historia del pueblo mapuche: Siglo XIX y XX. Santiago, Chile: Ediciones Sur.

Comisión de Verdad Histórica y Nuevo Trato con los Pueblos Indígenas. (2003). Informe de la Comisión Verdad Histórica y Nuevo Trato de los Pueblos Indígenas. Santiago de Chile: Gobierno de Chile.

Correa Agurto, P. (2014). Nace una voz: La huelga de hambre de los presos políticos mapuche y el testimonio de Natividad Llanquileo. Santiago de Chile: Ediciones Radio Universidad de Chile.

Instituto Nacional de Derechos Humanos. (2014, July 30). CorteIDH condena al estado de Chile por aplicación de ley antiterrorista a dirigentes mapuche. Noticias INDH. Santiago de Chile.

Llanquileo, N. (2009). Algo de mí [Blog]. Retrieved from https://www.blogger.com/profile/10387937447595644454

Mapuexpress. (2011, February 22). Cuatro Mapuches declarados culpables en el juicio de Cañete. Mapuexpress. Santiago de Chile. Retrieved from http://www.mapuexpress.net/content/news/print.php?id=6579

Totoro, D., & Retamal, I. (2011). Ngüenén: El engaño. Documentary, Ceibo producciones.

Fernanda Soler-Urzúa, McGill University, Montreal, Quebec, Canada

Michelle Harazny, Activist Artist, Regina, Saskatchewan, Canada

Chapter 9

Dylan Mahlingham, US

Social Enterprise and Web-Based Relief Initiatives

Shirine Aouad

Dylan Mahalingam is a nineteen-year-old American philanthropist and social entrepreneur born on August 2, 1995. Dylan's projects focus on youth empowerment and international development across the globe. His largest-scale initiative is the formation of Lil' MDGs in 2004, when he was nine years of age. Lil' MDGs is an organization whose mission centers around furthering the United Nations' (UN) Millennium Development Goals (MGDs) in developing countries by leveraging the internet, as well as digital and social media platforms.

Early Life
Dylan Mahalingam, was born Krisna Mahalingam in New Hampshire, USA. He was born to Indian parents, first-generation immigrants that left India for the United States in search of a better quality of life.

Growing up as part of a middle-class family in the United States, Dylan did not experience first-hand racial bias or discrimination based on his ethnicity, notably due to the fact that he was raised in a primarily Hindu community in New Hampshire. Nor did Dylan Mahalingam, raised as a vegetarian, experience poverty or want, although his parents sensitized him to the realities of world hunger.

From a very young age, Dylan recalls that his mother consistently insisted that he finish his plate, lest any food go to waste. Dylan's mother in fact often reasoned with her son that his leftovers represented a week's worth of food for families in less fortunate conditions. Despite Dylan's reluctance to comply, he recalls seriously contemplating ways—at the tender age of three—to avoid overeating as well as to "to get the food on my plate onto the plate of someone else who needed it."

In school, Dylan favored math and sciences. He is remembered by his teachers as a bright student, going on to rank first in a class of 707 students at the time of his graduation from Pinkerton Academy. He also engaged in a wide variety of both musical and athletic extracurricular activities, learning to play traditional Indian instruments such as the mrdanga and kartals and eventually going on to earn a black belt in karate.

Turning Point and Inspiration

In 2003, at the young age of eight, Dylan traveled to Chennai in India with his family. During this trip, Dylan was exposed to the socioeconomic realities of a developing country for the first time, which made a lasting impression. So lasting in fact that Dylan was able to recount the trip in great detail some nine years later, in 2012, in the *Huffington Post* article "Tiny Hands at Work Before Their Time":

> At the age of eight, I witnessed firsthand on a family trip to India the realities of poverty. I saw families struggling with the daunting task of finding food for their kids.

During this trip, Dylan met Madhvi, a six-year-old girl working in a brickyard alongside her parents in order to help pay off her grandfather's debt of 6,000 rupees ($120 USD). He also met Sumathi, who at 13 years-old was working as an "ayah" or nanny for a wealthy family for a meager 1,200 rupees ($23.50 USD) a month.

Upon returning to the United States, Dylan pursued his newfound interest in the relief of poverty, turning to technology—a long-standing hobby—as a means of raising funds. Along with a group of students from various New Hampshire schools, Dylan launched an educational website which went on to raise $780,000 USD for tsunami relief following the 2004 Indian Ocean earthquake and tsunami.

Dylan recalls that he and his partners worked remotely on building the website, never meeting one another in person. Their success in "leveraging the collective power of youth using the internet, assured [Dylan] that age [is] never an impediment to making a difference."

Lil' MPGs

Inspired by this first success, Dylan sought the opportunity to pursue organizing relief initiatives.

> After seeing how small actions on our part can help the most marginal and vulnerable kids worldwide to realize their full potential, I am inspired to continue to provide the tools and resources they need to make their dreams come to fruition.

That same year, at only nine years old, Dylan Mahalingam went on to found Lil' MDGs in collaboration with several cousins living across the United States. Lil' MDGs was founded as a non-profit organization with the objective of "unifying the giving power of youth using the internet and social and digital media to forward the UN Millennium Development Goals (MDGs)."

The eight Millennium Developments Goals (MDGs)—which include the eradication of extreme poverty and hunger and halting of the spread of HIV/AIDS, malaria and other diseases—constitute a globally endorsed program for the improvement of living conditions in developing countries.

The organization's official mission statement reads as follows:

> Lil' MDGs mission is to leverage the power of the internet, digital, and social media to educate, engage, inspire, and empower youth in all corners of the world to meet the MDGs.

Through Lil' MDGs' initiatives, Dylan was able to reach out to the very children in India that initially inspired him to become involved in relief initiatives. By providing training, tools and resources, the organization enabled Madhvi's family to acquire and run a tea stall, allowing them to provide for their family. Furthermore, Lil' MDGs provided Sumathi with the required training and inventory to pursue her interest in tailoring.

The organization's initiatives, however, did not stop at improving the lives of Madhvi and Sumathi. Beyond raising $780,000 USD for tsunami relief in its first year of existence, Lil' MDGs has raised over $10 million USD in hurricane relief since 2005 by mobilizing children from over 40 countries.

In collaboration with the UN Development program, Lil' MDGs has raised funds to build a school dormitory in Tibet, amongst a long list of other initiatives, including computer facilities, a library and a hospital in India, as well as "clean gravity-fed water systems in remote villages in Uganda."

Perhaps most impressively, Lil' MDGs has been able to mobilize and unify the efforts of over three million children across the globe in order to bring about change for over one million people worldwide.

> What I have discovered is that children want to help and get involved, and most of them find it fun, fascinating, rewarding, and less intimidating to use technology to accomplish this. Lil' MDGs is making it possible for them to do both.

In 2008, the United Nations recognized Lil' MDGs as the "best practice in e-content and technological creativity," and invites Mahalingam to be a youth speaker for its organization. Dylan has since resigned from his position as CEO of Lil' MDGs, stepping down in November of 2013. Today, Lil' MDGs is an initiative of Jayme's Fund. Dylan remains involved in Lil' MDGs' activities as a consultant.

A Unique Approach to Relief Initiatives

"I have always been fascinated with technology and the power of the internet. [Lil' MDGs] has been fortunate to capitalize on the fact that the internet is an excellent communications medium and we have used Facebook, Twitter, secure online forums, and YouTube, to name a few, to develop dialogues between our organization and our target audience."

Dylan's highly technological approach to the organization of relief has contributed to the development of a global community of empowered youth, whose impact has been magnified by international and interinstitutional collaboration. Online platforms have not simply enabled Lil' MDGs to mobilize funds and resources,but have also served to disseminate awareness of global issues across the globe.

> We began using these social media platforms to spread awareness to our target group. In addition, we have also shared facts about global issues, including childhood poverty, at conferences that we have attended in various countries.

Beyond his role as CEO of Lil' MDGs, Dylan has pursued this approach throughout a variety of other roles and initiatives.

Other Initiatives and Roles

Dylan founded *Green Your Lives* in 2009, an organization whose objectives include increasing public awareness of environmental issues and promoting green initiatives. This project led him to receive several awards, including the President's Environment Award from President Barack Obama.

That same year, Lil' MDGs continued success enabled Dylan to join the Nestlé Youth Foundation as a member of board. Also in 2009, Dylan was appointed Project Ambassador and Chief Strategist of Under the Acacia, an organization renowned for the scope of its African community projects.

In 2011, Dylan was awarded the Harris Wofford Youth Award by Youth Service America, which Dylan refers to as instrumental in allowing him to grow his philanthropic network and diversify his connections across industries and countries:

> The recognition opened up new doors and opportunities for me. I was able to network with executives from several organizations and businesses who have funded some of my projects in different countries. [...] This has helped me build new connections, allowing me to further expand our organization's reach toward meeting the UN MDGs.

In May 2012, Dylan was awarded the National All-Around Student Scholarship, a $2,000 college scholarship awarded to students who excel in three attributes favored by the Discus Awards. In Dylan's case, the scholarship was awarded as recognition for his "contributions to service, green, and academics."

Dylan has been a regular speaker for the United Nations since 2009. He continues to be involved in Lil' MDGs' initiatives as a consultant, with a focus on fundraising, management, and grant writing. He is also a panelist and a presenter for the United Nations Global Forum on information and communications technology and development.

Dylan was also the recipient of a four-year, full-tuition Foisie Scholarship for his Bachelor of Science in electrical and computer engineering at the Worcester Polytechnic Institute. He was also the recipient of the one-time Global Scholarship for Global Studies.

Projects

In a 2012 interview, Dylan discussed his plans for the future:

> I am interested in technology so I see that as a potential career choice for my future. [...] I anticipate continuing my work with Lil' MDGs and hope that I can find a program that would provide me with an opportunity to combine my intrinsic strengths with my interests.

He furthermore cites Arianna Huffington, President and Editor-in-Chief at The Huffington Post Media Group, Ban Ki-moon, former Secretary-General of the United Nations and Barack Obama as his influencers. Dylan was a software engineering intern at iRobot as of May 2014.

Quick Links

- "Dylan Mahalingam," Peter Horsfield, accessed July 28th 2014, http://www.thextraordinary.org/dylan-mahalingam
- "Discus Awards," Facebook Network, accessed July 28th, 2014, https://www.facebook.com/DiscusAwards
- "Dylan Mahalingam," LinkedIn Network, accessed July 28th, 2014, http://www.linkedin.com/in/dylanmahalingam
- "Dylan Mahalingam: TEDxTeen 2010", TEDxTeen, accessed July 28th 2014, http://tedxteen.com/speakers-performers/tedxteen-2010/63-dylan-mahalingam
- "Millennium Development Goals: Background," United Nations, accessed July 28th, 2014 http://www.un.org/millenniumgoals/bkgd.shtml
- "Tiny Hands At Work Before Their Time," Dylan Mahalingam, accessed July 28th, 2014 http://www.huffingtonpost.com/dylan-mahalingam/tiny-hands-at-work-before_b_1441726.html
- "Why We Are Here," Lil' MDGs Non-Profit Organization, accessed July 28th, 2014, http://www.lilmdgs.org/whywearehere/index.php
- "History," Lil' MDGs Non-Profit Organization, accessed July 28th, 2014 http://www.lilmdgs.org/whoweare/history.php
- "Impact," Lil' MDGs Non-Profit Organization, accessed July 28th, 2014, http://www.lilmdgs.org/whywearehere/impact.php
  "Who We Are," Lil' MDGs Non-Profit Organization, accessed July 28th, 2014, http://www.lilmdgs.org/whoweare/history.php
- "Where We Work," Lil' MDGs Non-Profit Organization, accessed July 28th, 2014 http://www.lilmdgs.org/wherewework/index.php
- "About Dylan," accessed July 28th, 2014, http://www.dylan-m.us/index.php

Shirine Aouad, Montreal, Quebec, Canada

Chapter 10

Kamilia Manaf, Indonesia

LGBTTIQ Rights Activism

Rima Arthar

Kamilia Manaf founded Institute Pelangi Perempuan (IPP, Women's Rainbow Institute) at age 25, with a mission to empower young queer women in Indonesia. Kamilia raises awareness through what she calls "edufuntainment": using youth clubs, movie screenings, poetry sessions, and easy-to-understand media (comic books, magazines) to give life to internationally agreed upon sexual rights and human rights amongst young queer women and the wider community.

Challenges to Organizing for LGBT Rights in Indonesia
Being lesbian, gay, bisexual, transsexual, transgendered, intersex, or queer (LGBTTIQ) in Indonesia is not illegal, nor has it ever been under Indonesian national law. Throughout Indonesia's history there have existed diverse communities within which LGBTTIQ identities have been respected and celebrated, in everyday life, in rituals and ceremonies, and in artistic cultural practices (songs, dances, plays) for hundreds of years. For example, the Bugi people of south Sulawesi recognize five gender expressions: woman, man, calalai, calabai, and bissu. Calalai are biological females who take on a masculine gender expression, and who tend to have romantic and sexual relationships with women throughout their lives. Calabai are biological males who take on a feminine gender expression, and who tend to have romantic

and sexual relationships with women throughout their lives. The bissu are transgendered people who are revered as spiritual leaders and guides within the Bugi communities.

In East Java, there is a historical dance, the Reog Ponorogo, which portrays a romantic relationship between the male characters of Warok and Gemblak. These are only a few examples of the ways in which diverse forms of gender expression and sexual orientation exist in Indonesian societies, and many more exist across other parts of the world.

However, as LGBTTIQ rights have become more visible as a political issue in Indonesia and elsewhere, there has also been a rising backlash against the expression of variant genders and sexual orientation. Across contexts, LGBTTIQ citizens are still marginalized and face discrimination in social life. Sometimes this takes the form of hate-crimes—acts of physical violence against LGBTTIQ people, for things such as simply holding hands or showing affection in public.

In Indonesia, because there is no law that officially protects LGBTTIQ people from violence committed against them, when violence does happen it can be very challenging to achieve justice. There can be a lack of sensitivity and understanding from law enforcement. This makes it hard to file a police report, to have the police follow through with an official investigation, or to have a court trial that will bring the perpetrators to justice.

Beyond challenges with law enforcement, there are also not enough resources invested in education about LGBTTIQ rights by the Indonesian government state services. As a result, LGBTTIQ rights are not taught or discussed in public schools, which means there is a lack of education, awareness and welcoming environments for LGBTTIQ youth.

Another challenge to raising awareness is the issue of internet censorship in Indonesia. In the last few years, there have been many cases where websites that have resources about sexual health and sexual rights have been blocked by internet service providers. This has the double impact of restricting people's access to information and access to education, both of which are universal human rights. It is within this context that Kamilia Manaf began her organizing activities. Besides opening Institute Pelangi Perempuan (IPP) to for young LGBTTIQ women, Kamilia also helped found Indonesia's first woman-only boxing club for survivors of violence. She continues to carry out research projects to document the experiences of LGBTTIQ peoples' struggles in Indonesia, and also gives workshops and talks locally and internationally on sexual rights for youth and women particularly.

Biography

Kamilia Manaf was born in 1981 and grew up in a small town in the province of Lampung, located on the southern tip of the island of Sumatra, in Indonesia. At the age of 18, she left her hometown to study public relations and communications at the University of Lampung. *The following text is based on a Skype interview with Kamillia Manif, which took place September 19, 2014.*

For the first few years of life on campus, Kamilia shied away from the campus groups that organized around human rights issues. She felt alienated from them: How did human rights connect to her personal life and those of her friends? What difference did human rights make in the world around her? How would they relate to the work she wanted to do in the field of communications?

It was not until Kamilia met a young professor, Ikram Baadilla, who was also involved in local community organizing, that her perspectives began to change. Ikram was a board member of DAMAR (Women's Advocacy Institute), the only women's rights non-governmental organization (NGO) in Lampung at the time. DAMAR was also the only organization openly friendly to LGBTTIQ people in Lampung. He encouraged Kamilia, who could speak both Bahasa and English, to volunteer with the organization as an ESL teacher. She did so, but soon after began to take a keen interest in some of the more political programming that DAMAR undertook. She was encouraged to volunteer with those projects as well. Through volunteering, Kamilia began to learn about the importance of international human rights, the challenges that women and girls faced being particularly targeted for violence, and how raising awareness on LGBTTIQ rights was directly connected to anti-violence and anti-oppression work. She would attend workshops, record and transcribe interviews, facilitate conversations as a translator, and write newsletters on the community organization's activities and their impacts. She began to see how organizing for human rights created tangible change in the world around her, and she was inspired to connect her communications skills to advocacy efforts.

Encouraged by her professor, in 2004 Kamilia decided to move to Yogyakarta, the second largest city in Indonesia, to pursue an internship with INSIST!, an LGBTTIQ-friendly organization. She remembers attending her first workshop with them and being pleasantly surprised—it was the first time she had seen so many LGBTTIQ people in one room. While the majority of the participants were gay men, Kamilia felt for the first time that she was in a space where she was completely welcome and able to be herself without fear of discrimination. That workshop was pivotal in shaping Kamilia's desire to create more safe spaces for her own community, and to raise the political consciousness of society in guaranteeing respect and non-discrimination for LGBTTIQ people.

Inspired by her experiences with INSIST!, Kamilia moved to Jakarta, the capital city of Indonesia, in late 2004. She wanted to continue working with progressive community organizations and to develop more links with like-minded activists. As a metropolis, Jakarta is an urban center that draws a lot of people from smaller towns in search of economic and social opportunities, and is also an interconnected hub where social justice-oriented, non-profit community organizations and NGOs are located.

Kamilia soon began working as a radio journalist with Yayasan Jurnal Perempuan (YJP, Women's Foundation for Journalism). In that space, Kamilia found a platform to raise awareness and create dialogue in the form of radio programming. She began interviewing people about their experiences, writing articles and hosting radio spots to debate current issues, particularly related to women's rights and anti-violence advocacy. She also learned the importance of having a critical understanding of the media—the way that it can slant social perspectives in favor of certain political interests—and the importance of engaging with media to both participate in conversations and to change them. Learning from older mentors and experienced activists is one of many ways to explore and engage with community organizing. Kamilia's advisors—her professor Ikram and the women she worked with at YJP—played a big role in encouraging her to start her own projects and to find out what she felt were the most pressing issues for her community. They also helped put her in touch with people who might support her work.

Figuring out the Needs of LGBTTIQ Youth

By the time Kamilia finished her internship with YPJ, she was 24 years old. At the time, there was no organization that focused specifically on the challenges faced by young LGBTTIQ women. According to Kamilia, youth are especially vulnerable because they are dependent on their families and caretakers. That dependency limits the choices they can make for themselves. Girls generally face more barriers to accessing education, entering the workforce, and living independently than their male counterparts. As a result, a common challenge for LGBTTIQ youth is feeling their lives are out of their control, that they are unable to make their own decisions, and fearing rejection and the loss of housing, education, income and community support if they are open about their gender identities and sexual orientation. Another pressure is a somewhat pervasive idea that LGBTTIQ youth under the age of 18 are 'fixable,' as if they are 'just going through a phase' and should be pressured to reform. This pressure is made worse by a lack of available information and resources aimed at youth, including information about the connection between human rights and the right to freely express one's sexual orientation and gender identity.

Kamilia Manaf has recounted that she herself faced discrimination and homophobia as a youth from one of her teachers, which made her feel silenced. She didn't feel that she had the right to stand up against the discrimination, because her teacher—a figure of authority—made discriminatory comments. There was no welcoming space for discussion in her school, and she had never been taught about human rights, nor had she been taught about the differences between 'sex' and 'gender' and 'sexual orientation.' In very simple terms, sex (female, male, intersex) is an identity assigned to everyone at birth, based on the biological characteristics (sexual organs, hormone levels, bone size, etc.) one is born with. One can change their sex through various means, including taking hormone supplements and surgery.

Gender is how one chooses to express their identity, based on ideas of the 'normal social roles' for women and men. One might be born female, and choose to identify as a girl/woman. One might be born male, and choose to identify as a girl/woman. Or one might choose to transcend these categories. There are numerous ways to express one's gender identity.

Sexual orientation is an expression of whom one is attracted to physically and romantically. An important point about sex, gender and sexual orientation is that they can change in a person's life. It is up to an individual to choose how to express themselves in their bodies in a way that feels true for them.

It wasn't until Kamilia moved away from her small rural hometown that she gained access to these ideas. Through her work with YJP, Kamilia came into contact with many other young lesbian and gay women activists who had similar experiences, and who were also looking to start their own projects. Something that resonated widely amongst Kamilia and her friends was the paramount need to have access to information—about civil, social, economic and human rights, sexual health, and LGBTTIQ experiences—as a young person. They felt that if they had this information and the ability to openly discuss the issue, it would have allowed them as youth to develop more confidence and self-assurance, to stop living in denial and feeling silenced, and to develop a network of allies and support going forward. Through these discussions, the idea for Institute Pelangi Perempuan (IPP) was formed.

Starting Institute Pelangi Perempuan:
Informal Collective Organizing

IPP started off as an informal collective project. Kamilia and the collective members first began organizing using online spaces, such as internet chat rooms and networking sites, as a meeting point. At the time, the internet was a common public space that felt safe for young urban lesbians to go actively seek out information and connections, for example through chat forums, or dating sites, or common-interests groups. As their online community connections grew, and the interest in organizing social events also grew, Kamilia and the collective members decided to use what they had available: turning coffee shops, people's apartments, and parks and other public spaces into gathering spots for discussions about their lives and experiences. The gatherings started off small and often stayed that way.

Kamilia recalled that first workshop where all of the participants were LGBTTIQ people and how it made her feel at home, and completely okay to be who she was in public for the first time. Finding community and creating safe spaces where people can express themselves, their thoughts, their emotions and desires freely is not something that everyone has access to. IPP started off by simply bringing people together in a welcoming environment. Badminton, for example, is a favorite pastime in Indonesia. IPP members would organize badminton games in the parks, after which those who attended would share dinner and just hang out. The idea of keeping things fun, offering support to individuals, and combining socializing with awareness raising was always at the center of what became IPP's motto: 'education, fun, and entertainment,' or 'edufuntainment.'

One of the first ways of having a more critical discussion was having film screenings of popular movies that portrayed LGBTTIQ characters and experiences. Kamilia and friends would go to the markets, scouring the DVD bins for anything that might relate, and building up a collection for these monthly screenings. After showing the film, the group would spend some time reflecting on what they had seen. How were the characters depicted? How did the films they found, which were often from foreign (Chinese, European, American) cinema, resonate with their lives in the Indonesian context? What were some of the positives and negatives of the storylines? The film screenings became a launching point to discuss how to positively impact the representation of LGBTTIQ peoples, and to recognize how media (newspapers and shows, films, advertisements, pop songs, music videos, etc.) influences our ideas about social 'norms' and behaviors.

Becoming a Formal NGO

As the events became more popular, the collective started building bigger alliances, and inviting feminist activists to events who could also share their organizing experiences and facilitate critical discussions. In late 2005, after about a year of informal organizing, the collective members discussed turning IPP into a formal NGO. With only about four active organizers, IPP was in need of extra resources in order to sustain its activities. On the one hand, becoming an NGO would bring new bureaucratic challenges, make the friendships between people more formal and professional, and change the structure of IPP's organization. However it would also allow them to apply for grants, establish a formal presence and take a somewhat public stand for LGBTTIQ rights.

As the first group of its kind focused on young LGBTTIQ women, IPP attracted the attention of older activists who wanted to support its growth. The Global Fund For Women—a philanthropist organization that supports grassroots feminist activism particularly in Asia, Latin America, Africa and the Middle East—was the first to offer financial support. With their successful grant application, IPP was able to open an office in Jakarta, offer part-time salaries for its three staff members, and pull together a board of directors consisting of older activists who could offer strategic guidance. IPP's activities expanded rapidly in the next few years:

- IPP started 'Lez School,' a short course on gender, sexuality, feminism and LGBTTIQ rights taught through field trips, music and poetry sessions, and game nights.

- IPP also helped start Kartini Sejati, Indonesia's first women's boxing club for survivors of violence, based on a project model that had worked well in other countries. Like their other activities, the club provided another safe space in which to hang out, work through traumatic experiences, and build physical and emotional strength and resilience.

- IPP also found creative ways to distribute their information, such as using invite-only LISTSERVs, and handing out newsletters on burned CDs that had regular album covers on them so as to not draw unwanted attention.

The Yogyakarta Principles Comic Book

One of IPP's more well-known projects is *The Yogyakarta Principles* comic book. *The Yogyakarta Principles* are a declaration about the sexual rights that every individual is entitled to under international law—whether lesbian, gay, bisexual, transgendered, transsexual, intersex, queer or heterosexual—the rights apply equally to everyone. Yet international law is written in a language that many young people cannot access, and the UN official languages into which the declaration was originally translated do not include Bahasa Indonesia.

Kamilia decided to write a youth-friendly book that would explain how these principles apply in everyday life, in easily accessible language and images. IPP reached out to researchers, activists and artists to plan the project, and interviewed 12 young lesbian women about their struggles (ranging from social discrimination, to being rejected by their families, to the way that homophobia is internalized) as well as the strategies they used to overcome these barriers. They amalgamated these stories into the comic book, drawn by a local artist and written in Bahasa Indonesia. They launched it at a community event that included dance and theatre performances, and was mostly attended by their allies and the young women who came to IPP events.

Unexpectedly, the comic book became something of a catalyst for connecting IPP to the broader human rights movement. After the launch, news of the comic spread first within IPP's networks in Indonesia. IPP was invited to speak at a feminist Islamic boarding school in what was a more conservative town. There were concerns that other orthodox religious organizations in the town might protest, but the event was a success and helped raise awareness that whatever one's religious background, human rights and sexual rights belong to everyone as an individual.

After that, Kamilia was invited to a regional feminist conference to share the comic with international activists, who felt that the comic had a lot of potential as an international teaching tool. She met members of the International Lesbian, Gay, Bi, Trans and Intersex Association (ILGA), who invited Kamilia to share the comic at the UN Commission on the Status of Women (UN CSW) in New York. There she was able to connect with groups who offered to provide funds to translate the comic into English, French and Dutch, and to distribute the comic internationally.

Making Use of International Support

The success of the comic was in some ways a turning point. It enabled Kamilia and other IPP members to attend workshops where they could gain new skills in advocacy and strategic planning. They were also invited to forums where policy decisions are made, and had the opportunity to connect with high-level decision-makers. The solidarity and support of international networks was very important, especially when the atmosphere within Indonesia became more hostile to LGBTTIQ rights.

When the comic was launched, even within the conservative religious town, IPP did not face threats to their personhood. In 2008 however, the Indonesian government passed a law that criminalized the publication of any information related to 'sexually suggestive performance' or so-called 'immoral acts', and LGBTTIQ groups were negatively impacted by this legislation. When Kamilia and others were organizing the fourth Regional Conference on LGBT rights in Surabaya, Indonesia in 2010, a large number of protestors from extremist groups intimidated the organizers and threatened violence on the first day of the conference. Fearing for the safety of the conference participants, organizers had to cancel the event. With the help of their international networks, however, IPP was able to offer new trainings on digital security and organizing security for LGBTTIQ activists in Indonesia.

IPP

In 2005, IPP was the first grassroots organization of its kind in Jakarta. Since then, it has helped create a more welcoming environment for a youth-friendly movement on sexual rights and LGBTTIQ rights in Indonesia. IPP began as a fun and informal project, when a group of friends got together and decided to create safe spaces for their community. They started with games, poetry, music and fun activities, and they continue with that today. Even when there is more backlash against LGBTTIQ rights, and there are more physical security threats, IPP manages to sustain its work. This is partly helped by having the chance to connect to an international human rights movement, but mainly due to the dedication of local organizers.

Keeping their youth-friendly edufuntainment focus is still a top priority for IPP, even though today the original members are over 30 years old. Kamilia is now investing a lot of time in using the spaces and networks she has created to empower a new generation of young queer activism in Indonesia, and particularly providing support to collectives in more rural areas. She continues to conduct research on LGBTTIQ rights, to create fun publications and harness the internet and social media to raise awareness, and also gives talks and workshops internationally.

Quick Links

Links related to IPP and Kamilia's story

- See this map for a short introduction to diverse sex and gender identities across the world: http://www.pbs.org/independentlens/two-spirits/map.html

- *Yogyakarta Principles* comic book by IPP (English): http://www.slideshare.net/pelangiperempuan/komik-english-2a

- An interview with Kamilia Manaf (MP3 download): http://www.isiswomen.org/index.php?option=com_phocadownload&view=file&id=323:kamilia-manaf-ilga-panel-2&Itemid=243&start=20

- Institute Pelangi Perempuan's website (Bahasa Indonesia): http://www.pelangiperempuan.or.id/

- Choice for Youth & Sexuality's official definitions of sexual and reproductive health rights: http://www.choiceforyouth.org/information/sexual-and-reproductive-health-and-rights/official-definitions-of-sexual-and-reproductiv

Links to Youth-Friendly Resources on Sexual Health and Sexual Rights (Canada)

- Youth Line Canada: http://www.youthline.ca/index.php

- Native Youth Sexual Health Network: http://www.nativeyouthsexualhealth.com/

- Queering Sex Ed: http://queeringsexed.com/

- Egale Canada: http://egale.ca/

Rima Athar, Coalition for Sexual and Bodily Rights in Muslim Societies (CSBR), Surabaya, Indonesia

Chapter 11

Tamer Shaaban, Saudi Arabia/Egypt

Human Rights Activism

Hala Kamaliddin

Although he was born in Buffalo, New York, Shaaban spent most of his life in Saudi Arabia with frequent visits to his parents' homeland, Egypt. At the age of 16, Shaaban visited the Egyptian pyramids, where he shot his first experimental film with his father's old handycam. Ever since then, he's been intrigued by the idea of combining technology and film to create thought-provoking stories.

Born to a software engineer (father) and an agricultural engineer (mother), Shaaban decided to study computer science. In May 2011, he completed a bachelor's degree in computer science at the Georgia Institute of Technology, in Atlanta, Georgia, U.S.A., during which he studied film and spent a year in Cairo studying physics and psychology.

During his studies, Shaaban also founded Mantis Films, where he created independent films that earned him multiple awards and international recognition. He was named one of YSA and the *Huffington Post*'s 25 Most Powerful and Influential Young People in the World, nominated for a *Forbes*' 30 Under 30, and was an Honorary Speaker for the Amnesty International Annual AGM and a Microsoft Thinkweek published author. At the age of 22, Tamer Shaaban became a global activist for publishing a video on the 2011 Egyptian revolution. Backed with technical expertise and a passion for positive change,

Shaaban is an award-winning filmmaker with projects on gender equality and human rights.

Activism Ignited

On January 25, 2011, tens of thousands of people marched to Tahrir Square in Cairo, Egypt, demanding the then-president of the republic, Hosni Mubarak, to step down. Mubarak, who ruled the country for 30 years, deployed the army to crush the protests, only to drive more Egyptians to the streets. People set up camp in Tahrir Square. Clashes ensued between government forces and protestors. Thousands were injured and arrested. Eighteen days later, on February 11, protesters marched to the Presidential Palace, forcing Mubarak to finally step down, granting the Egyptian people what they had so long desired.

It was on that 'Day of Revolt' that 22-year-old Egyptian-American filmmaker, writer, blogger, and actor Tamer Shaaban dove into news footage of the uprising. "I remember those streets in Cairo, where it all happened," he says. The result was a 2:15-minute video montage that reflects Egyptians' frustrations with the ruling regime. Moved to tears by their plight, Shaaban decided to post his film online. It went viral. Over two and a half million people watched the film. It was shared on YouTube, Reddit, Facebook and Twitter. News organizations around the world featured the film, including the *Huffington Post*. People wanted to know the activist behind the video. It was through his film, amongst the many efforts of other Egyptians, that carried the voices of the uprising in Egypt, and helped them echo across the globe.

Shortly after the publication of Shaaban's film, the video was banned in Egypt. He was prohibited from entering the country, a ban that was lifted after Mubarak's resignation. The young filmmaker never spoke out against Mubarak, though; he merely showed the struggles of the Egyptian people under the dictator's regime. Shaaban's focus is to give those problems a 'face'. "We can connect better with the individual than the mass," he says.

Three days after the Egyptian uprising, one of Shaaban's friends and a relative, a 27-year-old Egyptian, was leaving a hospital after a lengthy illness when he was caught in the line of fire and shot at point-blank range in the street. "He's my hero," says the filmmaker. This incident inspired Shaaban to shoot his next film, *The World Calls for Peace*. This 2:20-minute video shows people from different ethnicities voice their support for Egypt and the desire for peace in their native languages. Ever since its inception, *The World Calls for Peace* has been viewed over 264,000 times.

Refusing to limit himself with political causes, Shaaban expanded his films to include education and women's right, particularly issues pertaining to sexual violence.

While in seventh grade in Saudi Arabia, a teacher read a news story to Shaaban's class about a rape case that took place in India, a story that remained with the filmmaker for years to come. After discovering more stories of similar cases later on, Shaaban decided to produce a film to raise awareness on the issue. *Whispers of Shaitan* is a 2011 Mantis film based on a true story where four teenage boys take a test of manhood too far. The five-minute video, translated into Hindi, is about rape in India and the consequences perpetrators have to live when committing such a heinous crime, especially in the case of young offenders. "This was one of the most difficult projects I've ever done," says Shaaban.

The filmmaker's approach is to deliver such stories in a format suitable to audiences of all ages. He believes a clean video that focuses on the message without showing violence and geared towards awareness will encourage viewers to partake in positive impact. *Whispers of Shaitan* earned Shaaban the 2011 Best Picture–Campus Movie Fest Award at the Georgia Institute of Technology and has been watched by more than 12,000 viewers online.

As is the case with a lot of his videos and documentaries, Shaaban combines innovative technology with film, motivated by the idea of reaching global audiences to educate about human rights and the potential to become active agents towards a better future for their communities. "Don't be a keyboard activist," he says.

For instance, Shaaban and his 29-year-old sister Deana, a fashion designer, are currently working on a film project showcasing the achievements of Egyptian women. The film includes profiles of the only female pilot in the country, a female motorcyclist and an industrial designer—all dressed in Deana's creations. The key message here is empowering women regardless of where they come from. "We've been conditioned often to see women in a specific role," he says. Things are beginning to shift in terms of gender equality in Egypt, according to Shaaban, especially now that more people are speaking up against sexual harassment and rape. This film will be in English to reach a wider audience since Shaaban believes in connecting people and spreading awareness on a global scale. To him, you start in education. "To get anywhere, [one has] to fail first," he says, but these missteps are not failures to the filmmaker, rather a necessary element in the development process.

To Shaaban, film is a unique medium that can reach all audiences and can be an effective tool that transcends geographical boundaries. "Not everyone needs to be literate to understand film," says Shaaban. Film can teach people about how to respect one another, to take pride in one's country and identity, and gain a wider understanding of the challenges and achievements of other cultures.

Currently, Shaaban works with Microsoft on multiple projects for the public sector, including UNICEF and the World Bank. Despite the busy schedule he has with Microsoft, though, Shaaban sees this job as a hobby, his focus lying in inventions and ongoing projects for the non-profit sector. Some of his upcoming films cover the Egyptian revolution, the Palestinian/Israeli conflict, and war crimes. In terms of the latter, it is vital to dissolve stereotypes, such as ones surrounding Muslims, Arabs and immigrants as a whole, before educating people about conflict.

The young activist is also a contributor to *The Huffington Post*, where he's planning to integrate an in-depth, multimedia-type blog.

Additional Recognition and Awards

- Screening Atlanta Film Festival
- Screening Cannes Short Film Corner
- Screening Formula Mundi Film Festival
- Special Mention InterFilm Berlin
- Microsoft MVP Leadership Award
- Microsoft TechReady Most Innovative Solution Award
- Other films by Tamer Shaaban
- Ode to DC
- Silent Heroes
- The Battle Monument

Quick Links

- http://tamershaaban.com
- http://vimeo.com/tamershaaban
- http://www.bbc.com/news/world-middle-east-12327995 (context on Egypt uprising)

Hala Kamaliddin, Writer, Calgary, Alberta, Canada

Chapter 12

Natsuno Shinagawa, Japan

Raising Awareness and Getting Involved

Paul Chamness Miller

Natsuno Shinagawa became involved in UNICEF at the age of 11 by working with the organization's Childnet program, designed to increase Japanese youth's awareness of the world's problems. Her work with Childnet led to her studying in Africa, where she currently aids companies and organizations who are looking to engage in social activism.

According to Avert, a charity based in the UK, Africa is the most affected continent by human immunodeficiency virus infection/acquired immune deficiency syndrome (HIV/aids) with roughly 70% of the world's infections of the deadly disease. In 2012 alone there were 1.2 million new HIV infections and 1.6 million deaths. HIV has created a chain of social problems throughout Africa. The overall life expectancy has significantly shortened in several countries. Home life has also been severely affected; when the primary income provider falls ill, other family members must also quit working to care for ill family members. Children are also often forced to quit going to school to help care for ill family members or to earn money to make up for lost income. The disease has created a shortage of appropriate healthcare facilities and professionals, and has had a large impact on schools with increased absenteeism and a lack of teachers. This shortage of educators also leads to a lack of education, which is very instrumental in the prevention of deadly diseases like HIV.

In addition to the lack of education, there are a number of challenges that make battling this disease difficult. First, HIV diagnosis and lifetime treatment are very costly, which puts significant financial burdens on African countries and external world organizations that are striving to fight this disease. Living with HIV also carries a stigma, leading to discrimination. These negative attitudes among the public and healthcare providers prevents people from seeking diagnosis and proper care, and often leads to concealing their HIV status from others. Women are also particularly vulnerable to infection because of their social status in society. They often lack opportunities for education, and are often physically dominated by male sexual partners who deny them the option of engaging in safer sexual practices. Stigmas are also perpetuated in countries' criminalization of individuals who knowingly transmit HIV to someone else, even from mother to baby in some countries.

As Natsuno Shinagawa discovered, many Japanese youth lack awareness of what is going on in the world. This may be partially because Japan is an island. Sometimes people living on an island, especially youth, feel separated from the rest of the world and do not feel connected to the world's problems. However, youth have the power to bring about change and make the world a better place. The world will become a better place if youth will get involved in solving the world's problems. Natsuno did just that by becoming involved in UNICEF's (United Nations International Children's Emergency Fund) program, Childnet, designed to increase awareness of Japanese youth. As Natsuno's dedication shows, all youth need to do is to learn about society's problems and find the resources to bring about change.

Natsuno was 11 when she first began to think about becoming an activist. It started with an article she read about street children in Southeast Asia. Reading this article sparked something in her, even though she didn't know what to do about it. In the upper corner of the article she read was a miniature poster for UNICEF, but it wasn't legible. In order to read the poster, she used a microscope from her science class, and discovered that there was a phone number for their office in Tokyo. She called them right away and told them, "Hi, my name is Natsuno, and I am a 5th grade girl who lives in Tochigi. I read about street children in a foreign country, and I want to do something. What can I do?"

This was the beginning of a life-changing experience for Natsuno. UNICEF sent her some materials about their organization and how to get involved, and they invited her to join their club for children, Childnet. The first event she attended was overwhelming, because she is from a countryside town called Tochigi, and most of the other members of the club were from

Tokyo, a very big city, and they seemed quicker, and more experienced, active and knowledgeable. Although she felt like a fish out of water, her curiosity kept her going, and she felt more comfortable being part of something bigger than herself.

What is Childnet?

Childnet is a division of UNICEF Japan whose goal is to raise youth's awareness of global issues. What is particularly great about this particular group is that it is organized and run by youth. For example, in 2006, around a dozen Childnet youth activists organized several seminars in Tokyo to help educate youth on HIV/AIDS and brainstorm ideas on how to fight this deadly disease. Out of these seminars the activists created fliers and presentations to share with others. They also came up with a list of points of action for adults and youth. Adults need to:

- Talk more about HIV/AIDS to their children
- Provide more information at school to help fight stigmas
- Create more hospitals and healthcare workers in affected areas
- Offer more media coverage that shares the reality of the disease
- Give more money to support the fight against the disease
- The Childnet team recommended that youth should:
- Talk about the disease and share experiences with friends and family
- Converse about HIV/AIDS at school
- Mentor other youth who want to learn more about how to help
- Engage in community activities where discussions about the disease can take place

What Did Natsuno Learn?

It was through these experiences with UNICEF that Natsuno began to realize that youth in Japan are not aware of the problems of the world. She also discovered that most adults underestimate the ability of youth to engage in world-changing events. Her activism began at home by addressing this lack of awareness. She started by organizing activities at her school in Tochigi to help her own classmates learn about the problems of the world. One such example was HIV/AIDS. She admits that she didn't really see how this deadly disease related to her, until she saw a video that described a young girl's family that was impacted by the illness and Natsuno realized that not many youth around her knew about the devastation this disease brings, so she organized sessions to teach her peers about this terrible situation (Li, 2005). She also became involved at a national level by organizing bi-annual UNICEF seminars throughout Japan that were geared for youth from 6 to 18 years old. As she developed her own knowledge and awareness, she participated in panels that were organized by UNICEF in Tokyo and even facilitated a Junior 8 (J8) Summit in Germany in 2007.

What is a J8 Summit?

A J8 Summit is a joint effort by UNICEF, Morgan Stanley, and the host country of the G8 Summit, which brings together dozens of youth from 14 to 17 years old (although 13-year-olds have also been invited) from each of the eight countries that participate in the G8 Summit, plus other youth from India, China, Brazil, Mexico and South Africa. The youth meet for one week to engage in workshops, roundtable discussions, and other activities to learn about world problems, discuss and debate them, come up with solutions and recommendations and be a voice in presenting their ideas to the G8 leaders, influencing these world leaders' decisions.

In 2007, the year that Natsuno participated in the J8 Summit, there were four topics the 74 youth tackled in their time together: HIV/AIDS, climate change and conserving energy, Africa's economy, and the global economy. At the end of summit, the youth drafted the "Wismar Declaration" in which they made several recommendations to the G8. They urged the G8 to increase funding to support fighting HIV/AIDS, as well as to see greater cooperation between Global Fund (part of G8) and other organizations, such as the Bill Gates Foundation and UNAIDS. Members of the summit also urged G8 leaders to consider their solutions to the economy in Africa, including the involvement of world banks, providing aid for better education, engaging with African organizations and offering funding to battle corruption of African governments and violence, and assisting in stimulating African businesses through loans and import tax relief, as well as increasing fair trade agreements. The youth also urged the G8 leaders to ensure that companies in Africa follow the principles of the UN Global Impact, designed to enforce social responsibility. Along with this social responsibility, they further suggested that human lives and well-being be given priority over financial gain in situations like patents, which have created serious limits in access to things such as HIV medication. Finally, in terms of global climate change, the J8 participants urged G8 leaders to develop incentives for businesses to use green technology, as well as committing to funding research initiatives related to green technology and making such technologies available to developing countries. They also expressed a desire to see greater education efforts made available to the public about climate change and energy efficiency. Lastly, they called on G8 leaders to take action on plans for reforestation and the preservation of forests.

It has been over 10 years since Natsuno started on her journey of activism, and it has completely changed her life. In particular, she began to think a lot about Africa, and the world's perception of this continent being neglected in terms of its poverty, health issues, among others, as well as its depiction of being a land of victimization. She began to question these perceptions and wanted to learn about these issues for herself. It was this desire that led Natsuno to participate in an exchange program for one year in Uganda as an undergraduate student. She learned from this experience that it is important to be a critical thinker, even about yourself and your own thinking, in order to become an effective activist.

Through her activism, Natsuno has met many people who have inspired her to keep going. She met her future professors at the university where she studied in Japan, as well as officials of the United Nations. These experiences motivated and drove to work even harder as a student and in her activism. Not only did they inspire her, but they also offered her a lot of advice to help her continue on her journey to bring about change in the world.

What is Natsuno Doing Now?

So where is Natsuno now? She is currently living and working in Dakar, Senegal in Africa. She works for a management consulting firm that focuses on international development, global issues and businesses in emerging markets. They offer support for many different kinds of organizations and institutions, including governments, non-governmental organizations (NGOs), international organizations and even private companies. Their goals to help these companies and organizations to make the world a better place. An example project that her company might do is to help a company start a business in rural Ethiopia so that they can sell nutritious bay food produced locally, helping to create sustainability in that community.

Although her work is meaningful, Natsuno realizes that there is still more work to be done back home in her homeland, Japan. In order to make a difference at home, she is working on her career as a writer so that she can continue to educate Japanese society about Africa, because as she says, "I strongly believe that we have a lot to learn from this continent."

Advice for Getting Involved

What is Natusno's advice to youth who might want to become involved in activism? She says that it is important that the motivation come from inside. She says that it is important that each future activist find the right cause or problem that he or she just cannot stop thinking about most of the time. If it's a topic that someone told the teenager to focus on, it may not be the right one. Once a topic begins to consume his or her every waking moment, then it is time to act on it. Natsuno recommends that youth begin by doing research first. They should look online (see resources below and throughout this book), contact organizations or people they find in their research, talk about the topic at home and at school, and be active in finding people who can help them become involved. Technology has made research much easier. Use search engines like Google to find out as much as possible about the topic, and take the initiative.

There are a lot of resources available to learn about youth involvement in fighting HIV/AIDS. For example, UNICEF partners with a lot of African organizations to help increase education among youth, who make up a large percentage of new cases of HIV. In Botswana, as an example, UNICEF joined forces with the Botswana government to create a program called Wise Up, specifically designed to educate youth about the risks and dangers of HIV. They use modern technology, like Facebook, to send messages to youth in order to teach them. This same program also teams up with you drama groups to help them develop their skills as artists and to create dramatic performances geared at educating children and youth not only about HIV/AIDS, but also about other problems their society is facing. Theater is a particularly powerful mode of communication, because is directly reflects society's behaviors and actions, and tends to have a longer-lasting impact on the audience, as well as the performers.

This inspiring story about Natsuno Shinagawa is but one example of how a single individual can have an impact on society. She allowed a story about what she learned in school to tug at her heart. Her humanity led her to find a way to share her life with others. It started in Japan, educating her own school and community, which afforded her a rare opportunity of joining other youth from around the world to help world leaders address important problems, followed by engaging in study abroad in Uganda. These opportunities gave Natsuno the experience she needed to do what she is doing now, continuing to help bring about change in Africa. Whether battling HIV speaks to you, or it is another problem in society, take Natsuno's advice and find some way that you can help make the world a better place, because the rewards are worth it.

Quick Links

Links related to Natsuno Shinagawa

- Story about Natsuno's work with UNICEF: http://www.unicef.org/infobycountry/japan_28010.html
- Podcast interview with Natsuno: http://www.podcastpedia.org/podcasts/1182/UNICEF-Podcast/episodes/546/Japan-Getting-young-people-involved-in-todays-world

Links related to youth involvement in world problems

- Junior 8 Summit (part of the G8 Summit): http://www.unicef.org/ceecis/ voice_children_6720.html
- Junior 8 Summit (USA): http://www.unicef.org/infobycountry/usa_44803.html
- UNICEF's main page: http://www.unicef.org
- Opportunities for youth: http://www.opportunitiesforyouth.org/
- Junior 8 Summit 2007: http://positivenews.org.uk/2007/archive/1099/junior-8-address-the-world/
- Wismar Declaration: http://www.unicef.org/ceecis/wismar_declaration_english.pdf
- Links related to HIV/AIDS in Africa
- Report about HIV/AIDS in Africa from Avert (UK): http://www.avert.org/hiv-aids-sub-saharan-africa.htm
- Childnet (Japan): http://www2.unicef.org:60090/aids/japan_35426.html
- HIV in Botswana: http://www.unicef.org/aids/botswana_71280.html

Paul Chamness Miller, Akita International University, Akita, Japan

Chapter 13

Specs & Veil, Canada

Film & Media Activism

Kayf Abdulqadir, Fartousa Siyad & Diane Watt

All three members of Specs & Veil, Kayf Abdulqadir, Fartousa Siyad, and Hodan Hujaleh are Somali-Canadian women who grew up in Ottawa. Kayf's interest in media started from an early age. Even before she had access to a camera, she remembers directing her younger siblings in the making of imaginary films. In her early teens she filmed some home videos and held small photo shoots with her friends. During high school she felt she didn't fit in, but that changed after she joined the movie club at her school. She also enrolled in a Media Studies class, which was paired with the Adobe Youth Voices Program. There she learned how to use camera equipment and also developed her editing skills. Kayf produced a short video called, *Fabric: The Unveiled Truth*. Her friend, Fartousa, makes a brief appearance in this film. In the summer of 2009, at the age of 18, Kayf's video won the Canadian title in a global Adobe Youth Voices contest and she was invited to attend an Adobe workshop at Stanford University in California with other winners from around the world.

Fartousa's teenage years were more focused on basketball and storytelling—books and ball! She was interested in media-making, but she didn't find her high school's media courses appealing. She felt disenfranchised from the curriculum and from her fellow students. She dabbled in photography in her senior year and during her first year of university, and created a photo series.

On December 17, 2011, the two friends were just hanging out and Fartousa showed Kayf the latest episode in a web series she liked called, *Awkward Black Girl*. The girls wondered whether any Somali media makers existed on YouTube. When they were unable to find anyone with their background making videos online they decided to create their own media company, Specs & Veil Productions. At the time, Fartousa wore "specs" and Kayf wore a hijab, so they thought this was a name to describe who they were. Little did they know at the time that their work would be so well received.

Less than ten days later, Kayf purchased a Canon HD DSLR camera, and on January 16, 2012 they uploaded their first video to YouTube—10 Types of Somali Girls. They came up with the idea for video in response to common stereotypes they were seeing in the mass media about Somalis and Muslim girls. What started out as a fun project for them and their friends to have a laugh ended up drawing international attention. Two days after being uploaded to YouTube they were offered a Google Adsense contract. The next day they were invited as guests on a local public radio program, *CBC Morning*, with Robyn Bresnahan. Their first YouTube video had gone viral, and overnight they had become media celebrities. By January 21, their first video was averaging 7,000 to 10,000 views a day! The girls received dozens of emails from other Somalis who loved their work and were pleased to finally see their perspectives represented in the media. Their work also proved inspirational. In the following days and months more and more videos made by Somali youth suddenly appeared on YouTube. Before being taken down three months later, 10 Types of Somali Girls had received 184,135 views. Their work obviously resonated with Somali youth worldwide.

The success of their first project opened doors for these two young filmmakers. They were invited to participate in a media program for minority youth sponsored by the United Nations Association in Canada, whose purpose is to link multimedia with multiculturalism. This initiative set out to examine and enhance the role that media plays in contributing to the inclusive representation of all Canadians. A few months later, in November 2012, Specs & Veil uploaded their second production to YouTube entitled, *Somali Problems*. In the first two years it received nearly half a million views. This video was also noticed by the mainstream media, and the girls were interviewed on the radio again. They were then invited to participate in a panel, Beyond the Soundbyte: A Public Panel on Independent Media and Diversity, sponsored by Women, Action & the Media and the United Nations Association in Canada's Multimedia and Multiculturalism initiative. In addition, they participated in a media internship, produced a promotional video for the Multimedia and Multiculturalism project, and attended a Knowledge to Action Forum to learn how to further develop their media-making skills to represent their views as youth from a marginalized community. Their most recent work consists of a web series on YouTube. The pilot episode of their production, *Chronicles of a Somali Girl* was posted in September, 2014, and after one month had nearly 2,500 views.

Hodan Hujaleh is the most recent member of Specs & Veil Productions. She brings her expertise as scriptwriter and actor to the team. In December 2014, Specs & Veil were invited to attend the PLURAL + 2014 Youth Video Festival Awards Ceremony at the Paley Center for Media in New York City, an event is sponsored by the United Nations Alliance of Civilizations (UNAOC), and the International Organization for Migration (IOM). Hodan and Kayf collaborated on a short video entitled, *Three Things You Should Know About My Hijab*, which won three international awards including the PLURAL+ Paley Center for Media Award, PLURAL+ Insight Film Festival Award and PLURAL+ Rai Educational Award. UNICEF also approached Specs & Veil and invited them to share their inspiring story with other young people around the world. Their success story has been published in the *Voices of Youth* website.

Specs & Veil were also invited to collaborate with Diane Watt, an educational researcher at the University of Calgary. They worked on a two-year project to share their story of media-making with other youth and educators. This included presentations at academic conferences, talks to teacher audiences, media workshops with high school students, co-publishing, and the production of an educational video on media-making and youth activism.

Their Motivations

Specs & Veil use humor in their videos as a means to battle stereotypes and humanize Somali individuals, who are generally represented in the mass media in limited ways. They pay careful attention to how mainstream media portrays non-white individuals and try to speak back to dominant meanings through their work. They also make videos to help provide for themselves and their families. When they first became involved in media-making, they did not see it as a way to earn a living, but now they consider it their career choice.

Kayf, Fartousa, and Hodan are motivated by their love of video and YouTube culture. However, this world is fast-paced and constantly shifting, and there is always the worry that if they don't get their material out quickly enough someone else may grab the spot they're coveting. They are constantly thinking about the next episode and the next project.

Their Service

Specs & Veil create videos for members of communities who feel alienated by traditional media. Growing up, they never saw themselves anywhere in the mass media or in the school curriculum. They are intent on creating narratives with voices that people don't usually hear. They challenge stereotypes about communities as well as norms set within and outside their respective cultures and communities related to women's roles in media and the workforce. They hope to provide opportunities for other Somali media makers by advertising their work through their networks and supporting them on their projects.

Hodan, Kayf, and Fartousa are committed to working directly with youth. They recently helped Diane Watt organize and lead a Media Club for a group of girls at a private Islamic high school. The students responded positively to having role models they could identify with—especially in the area of media-making. Specs & Veil look forward to mentoring other youth in the future through similar initiatives. By sharing their own stories and introducing video to other youth they will continue to have a positive influence in the future.

Where They Are Today

Specs & Veil are focused on building a larger portfolio and diversifying their interests. They continue to produce new episodes for their web series, *Chronicles of a Somali Girl*, and have also started the Street Fashion Ottawa photography project. They have been invited to work with youth in school and community settings and plan to pursue those opportunities.

Quick Links

Videos by Specs & Veil

YouTube Channel: http://www.youtube.com/user/specsandveil

1) *Sh*t Somali Girls Say*: (posted privately)

This is a Somali twist to the famous comedic skit, *S*it Girls Say* where an actor displays common lines a teenage Somali-Canadian girl would use. It was posted during the wave of *Sh*t Girls Say* videos that were trending on YouTube at the time.

2) *10 Types of Somali Girls*: (posted privately)

This video lists off 10 hilarious, exaggerated caricatures of Somali girls, including: Sporty Girl, Crazy Community Girl, Activist/Feminist, Hooyo's Girl, Gossip Girl, Thirsty Girl, Academic Brat Girl, Poet, and White Washed Ditz. This video is the one that brought Specs & Veil relative fame in the Somali YouTube sphere and attention from mainstream media outlets like the Canadian Broadcasting Corporation and Google.

3) *Somali Problems* (available on their YouTube channel):

This is a video detailing common Somali problems. Most are interactions between youth and their mothers or between friends. Many in the Somali diaspora really connect with this video, but Specs & Veil were most surprised by the response from non-Somali video watchers commenting that they've experienced or seen the same things happen in their communities.

4) *Somali Aabo* Teaser: (Vimeo)

A mock reality TV show following a Somali aabo (dad) through his everyday adventures. The Aabo signed up for the show by accident. He saw a sign on a table at the local supermarket and was attracted by the "easy money" line. The teaser shows what happened when the crew showed up to his house to start filming. He speaks entirely in Somali, stating his confusion and telling the crew to get off him. The actress behind this character is the talented Hodan Hujaleh, who is part of Specs & Veil as a second editor.

5) *Chronicles of a Somali Girl* Episode 1: (Available on their YouTube channel):

A series about an awkward Somali-Canadian university student and her quirky trials. The style is vlog/flashbacks and dramatic reenactments. The protagonist name is Fardowsa and the series is her chronicling her everyday trials and awkward encounters. Most interactions are set in a context where her Somali-Canadianness is at the center. For example, there's an episode planned where it's just a series of questions posed to her by her coworkers at the university newspaper office.

6) *Three Things You Should Know About My Hijab*: (Vimeo)

This quirky, humorous look at being constantly questioned about wearing hijab was produced by Hodan and Kayf in 2014. It has been recognized with three international awards and profiled on UNICEF's Youth Voices.

Social Media

Specs & Veil on Twitter: Specs&VeilProduction @specsandveil

Links and Connections

The amazing thing about how media is evolving and changing is that information surrounding how to get involved in media-making is literally at our fingertips. Fartousa, Hodan, and Kayf learned through their participation in their high school's media club project with Diane that youth much younger than them are faster at learning how to use media-making technologies and are the ones now teaching them about new methods.

In terms of the classroom environment, Specs & Veil recommend programs like Adobe Youth Voices be in every school. There are many benefits to giving youth the tools to tell their own stories. Whether it is a comedic skit, like what Specs & Veil have done, or a documentary piece about their communities, just creating something is a profound self-esteem-boosting experience. Media-making not only forces the individual to ask questions about how and why they're producing a piece, but also what lens they are using to view the world. Specs & Veil have learned a lot about their identities and how they want to disrupt stereotypes within their communities. They learned through producing videos, thinking critically about them after production, and then answering questions posed by others.

Making a difference is usually seen as something grand and flashy. For youth, Specs & Veil recommend programs like Adobe Youth Voices or the Multimedia and Multiculturalism UNAC (United Nations Association in Canada) program to help them figure out who they are. Media-making permits youth to explore what excites them and what passions they would like to pursue in terms of activism. Specs & Veil are living proof that youth making media can make a difference. Not only has their work impacted their own lives; they also continue to teach and inspire others.

Quick Links

- Adobe (2014). Adobe Youth Voices Program Guide. Waltham, MA: Education Department Center. Available at: http://cloudfront.youthvoices.adobe.com/2014/04/10/12/01/39/163/AYVProgramGuide_English_3.0.pdf

- Baudenbacher, G., Goodman, S. (2006). Youth-powered video: A hands-on curriculum for teaching documentary. (A resource from the Educational Video Center. New York, NY).

- United Nations Association in Canada (2012). The Multimedia and Multicultural Toolkit: A guide to understanding and using multimedia to build stronger communities through diversity in Canada. Available at: http://unac.org/wp-content/uploads/2013/10/TOOLKIT-mm-English.pdf

- United Nations Association in Canada (2011). Multimedia & Multiculturalism (M & M) Initiative. http://mmunac.org/about/

- Voices of Youth was founded in 1995 as UNICEF's "online place for young people to learn more about issues affecting their world. VOY was recently redesigned for a more modern youth audience and is now the go-to place where you can know more, learn more and do more about our world! You can share your thoughts and opinions with thousands of people from all over the world. You can also discuss social issues such as Education, Environment or Violence and Conflict and inform yourself about HIV/AIDS, Health or Human Rights." http://www.voicesofyouth.org

- Women, Action & the Media is "an international grassroots organization dedicated to building a robust, effective, inclusive movement for gender justice in media." http://www.womenactionmedia.org

Kayf Abdulqadir, Media Activist, Ottawa, Ontario, Canada

Fartousa Siyad, Media Activist, Ottawa, Ontario, Canada

Diane Watt, University of Ottawa, Ottawa, Ontario, Canada

Chapter 14

Matthew "Creeazn" Wood, Cree

First Nations Activism

Diana Pearson & Shima Robinson

Creeazn is an internationally recognized b-boy, DJ, grass dancer, Hip hop Kultural activist in Edmonton, Alberta, Canada. For a decade, he has been engaging youth in multicultural, postcolonial community-building and First Nations traditions through the elements of hip hop at a weekly event called CypherWild, in schools and on reserves across Canada.

First Nations' Struggles in Canada

People from all over the world have chosen to live on the land that First Nations (indigenous groups of Canada) people call Turtle Island, and European settlers call North America. In the part of Turtle Island called Canada there are many communities, and some of these communities are the nations of the indigenous people who have lived there for all time. The 630 First Nations in Canada are communities of people that have been historically mistreated and marginalized by the Canadian government. Their struggle has been long and hard beginning with European settlement in the 15th century.

European explorers reached Turtle Island by ship in 1492, and were greeted by Indigenous communities who helped them settle. These settlers began to build trade relationships with the indigenous peoples who were native to the land. The settlers used this new knowledge to make money. Some set out to reach Asia and India for trading purposes but instead landed on Turtle

Island. The explorers wanted to explore and expand their territory to gain power and resources. Upon reaching Turtle Island, trading networks were set up between the colonies and the Indigenous peoples. In the beginning the settlers brought diseases foreign to Indigenous peoples. They had no immunity. Unfortunately, some settlers used this to their advantage and traded diseased blankets for goods. They did this because settlers saw Indigenous culture as inferior. By 1871, treaties were negotiated between settlers and indigenous peoples. A treaty is a negotiation between two groups of people to ensure proper rights to share land and resources. Unfortunately, these were not upheld respectfully for Indigenous groups. The situation arising from European settlement on Turtle Island is known as colonialism. The colonialist mindset of the Europeans was the catalyst for many years of famine, war, mistreatment and cultural genocide of Indigenous peoples.

The Canadian government was eager to assimilate all First Nations and at the end of the 19th century opened residential schools. The Canadian government tore First Nations children from their families and forced them into an education system that had been designed to "get the Indian out of the child." First Nations children experienced severe cultural, physical, and sexual abuse. The effects of racism and the residential school system continue to impact the lives of First Nations people across the country in forms of post-traumatic stress disorders and other intergenerational trauma. Fortunately, the last residential school closed in 1996. Since then, there have been hopeful signs of community and cultural healing. The Truth and Reconciliation Commission of Canada (TRC) was established June 1st, 2008 with events taking place across the country for five years. The TRC was established to bring Canadian people of all backgrounds together to promote awareness of the struggle of First Nations people, and to begin to reconcile the injustice and trauma inflicted on First Nations people in residential schools. The goal of this awareness is to encourage community and cultural healing to make Canada a more inclusive and humane country. The 7th and final national TRC event took place March 27–30, 2014 at the Shaw Conference Center in Edmonton, Alberta.

The TRC is eager to promote reconciliation but many activists, both First Nations and settlers, are aware of the continuing inequality. The most popular and current resistance movement fighting for indigenous sovereignty and environmental rights and protections is Idle No More (INM). INM uses the tools of media, education, mobilization and civil disobedience. One of their goals is to counteract the interests of the oil industry that they see as being in partnership with the Canadian Government. INM has worked to organize First Nations citizens, their supporters and allies to march in the streets, hold flash mobs, observe traditional ceremony in public spaces, speak on the steps of the legislature building(s) and raise awareness online. Youth are central to this movement. They pass on the history and culture that the federal government has tried to suppress and eliminate. In order to do this, young First Nations street artists are becoming politically active, lending their voices and their art to cutting edge activism. For artists like Matthew "Creeazn" Wood, hip hop music is a tool in becoming idle no more.

Canada was founded on the treaties outlining the land rights and re-lations between First Nations and the Canadian government. Today, these treaties are verbally acknowledged by various levels of government and by the leaders of other groups but they are not being fully respected by Canadian law. Oil and other resource industries have been threatening the self-determi-nation of First Nations people. Indigenous ways of life are being threatened because these industries are spoiling their land in pursuit of profit. Edmonton is built on Treaty 6 land, as Creeazn reminds us at every weekly CypherWild gathering. His efforts to keep the young people aware are fundamental to the process of reconciliation and healing. Creeazn is not the only leader who hon-ors the history of Treaty 6, but his impact is greater because of his proximity to First Nations youth. His attention to the universality of hip hop culture and his emphasis of Cree heritage are a major draw for CypherWild. Creeazn's activism truly embraces a multicultural vision of Canada.

Biography
Matthew "Creeazn" Wood hosts a weekly event in Edmonton, Alberta called CypherWild during the spring and summer months. It is a free, all-ages event that uses the elements of hip hop (dancing, DJing, aerosol painting, MCing) to bring people of the Edmonton community together. At CypherWild, there is a strong feeling of creative energy. DJs spin beats. Both new and established MCs take their turn on the mic and are encouraged to practice storytelling in rhyme (cursing is discouraged). Local graffiti artists are welcome to paint canvasses on site. A cypher is made up of individuals who gather in a circle to practice their dance or rap skills. This circle formation and the sharing that occurs within it are traditional. CypherWild is a space where youth are encouraged to develop their creative talents through the elements of hip hop. Creeazn's activism welcomes people of all ages, ethnicities, backgrounds and skill levels to join in solidarity for the betterment of themselves and their community. Creeazn not only walks his talk, he dances it. As a b-boy and DJ, Creeazn is an activist for community health and he is struggling against centuries of oppression.

CypherWild

Creeazn created CypherWild to bring youth together to meet with their peers in a safe space very much like the founding Hiphoppas in New York, the Zulu Nation that created safe places where people can share their gifts. Cree is the name of one of the tribes of indigenous people living on Turtle Island. In traditional Cree culture, "gifts" are talents such as dancing, story telling, music and more. Keeping a safe place for creativity and for these gifts to flourish is the responsibility of the firekeeper. Creeazn emphasizes the importance of the role of firekeeper, (the term was brought to his attention by a fellow Indigenous b-boy, Q-Rock). The firekeeper's role is to keep the fire burning amongst community members, in other words to spark passion for community engagement. Creeazn accomplishes this through CypherWild. There, he encourages the passing on of the gifts of storytelling through elements of Hip Hop including dance, turntablism, aerosol painting and MCing. Using hip hop culture to encourage positive social change has been a very successful form of activism in the Edmonton community.

Creeazn recognizes the need for youth to have a sense of belonging, to fit in with their peers. Participation in CypherWild creates an opportunity for youth to gain confidence and to spark their creativity. Through the elements of hip hop, youth have a chance to express themselves and to share their personal stories. CypherWild is a space that provides a healthy sense of competition in a safe and non-threatening environment and helps to fight misconceptions about inner-city youth. Forty percent of the homeless population in Edmonton is Indigenous, and Indigenous youth make up a large portion of this number. Participating in CypherWild is a way to break down cultural barriers that lead to the creation of stereotypes of race, religion, and class that most negatively impact the most vulnerable people in our society. Creeazn works tirelessly to create and hold safe places free from the glorification of gang culture, crime, or underage drug and alcohol use.

Influences and Development of CypherWild

Creeazn is heavily influenced by Cree tradition. His mother was a major influence in his life from an early age, taking him to pow wows and teaching him about Cree culture and tradition. He went to school at Ben Calf Robe Elementary/Junior High where he had the opportunity to learn Cree language and culture through school programs. Creeazn thinks of creative energy as a frequency to be tapped into, like a radio in which you need to turn the dial to find the right station. He explains that both positive and negative frequencies can be received and that when youth are receptive to positive frequencies, they are less likely to engage in deviant behaviors such as crime and substance abuse, which are expressions of negative frequencies. Creeazn recalls that in his adolescence, he was "too distracted by the other frequencies to tap into the traditional frequencies of art, dance and creativity." It was his quest to tap into those traditional frequencies that led him to the realization that everybody is indigenous to somewhere and we can all learn from each other. These creative frequencies are now a central concept in his work at CypherWild, where he amplifies the positive frequencies for all attendees to tap into.

As he grew up he began to dance at various venues in Edmonton. Many of these venues were sober clubs, spaces where Edmonton youth would gather on the weekends for clean fun. One of these venues, Sports World, was a popular roller disco where street dancers would meet to show off their skills. His interest in both traditional dance and b-boying grew. Soon he and his fellow dancers were competing at youth dances. His internationally successful dancer friends, including James Jones, helped Creeazn by giving him opportunities to travel and dance with them. These opportunities put him in touch with a network of dancers with whom he would trade styles. He had the same experience with traditional dance, traveling to various pow wows meeting and trading styles with other dancers.

As a teenager, Creeazn began taking music lessons at the Boyle Street Education Centre while upgrading to graduate from high school. This music co-op program, of limited means, was lead by one of his mentors, Brett Lashua. With Brett's guidance, Creeazn and other students used one laptop, one mic and one turntable to create original music that they dreamed of refining and recording professionally. They amassed a collection of 5000 records in one small studio and built a recording booth in the back of their room. Creeazn has since nurtured and honed his skill as a turntablist and is known for his mixes and his presence in the community.

One of the early incarnations of CypherWild was known as Circle Strong as in "keep the circle strong." At these events Creeazn would not only dance but DJ as well, which came to him as second nature. Hip hop and traditional cultures share the roots of drums, music, dance, art and language. Circle Strong soon evolved into Hole 'Nother Level (HNL), a b-boy jam held at iHuman in Edmonton that was meant to keep the energy moving in his b-boy community. Creeazn noticed that people tended to only come out for the competitive side of dance, known as battling, which did not encourage positive social behavior. So he began to encourage a non-competitive cypher circle where members could improve their dance skills and share their story without fear of harsh judgment.

Creeazn has noticed many connections between Indigenous traditions and hip hop customs. He was inspired at a young age by Cree elder and Zulu Nation elder, Ernie Paniccioli, who is a world-famous hip hop photographer from Brooklyn, New York. Ernie has documented the history of hip hop through photography since the 1970's. Creeazn also makes the connection that both Indigenous and hip hop practices include drums, music, dance, art and language. Yet another parallel is that both breakers and traditional First Nations dancers dance in circles. It is the fusion of these influences that has led Creeazn to the creation of CypherWild.

The chosen name "Creeazn" stands for his Cree and Vietnamese heritage. Creeazn points out that everyone is indigenous from somewhere and that all of our stories need to be told in order to keep the circle strong. The international reach and appeal of traditional culture is exemplified in the Gathering of Nations (GON). Creeazn speaks with respect and excitement about his experience of dancing at the GON. The GON is a large annual pow wow that is held in Albuquerque, New Mexico, to which representatives of 500 Indigenous groups from Canada and the United States are invited to share their culture and dance together. Anyone can attend the GON whether or not they are Indigenous. In order to attend the GON 2011, Creeazn used $1400.00 in travel vouchers that he had won in a DJ battle to fly down to Albuquerque where he met up with some other dancers who had first connected to him through the internet or, as Creeazn puts it, recognized "the digital smoke signal." These dancers are part of a group called Chief Rockers who wear the logo "XFRX" in which the Xs stand for "meeting point from all directions." They all took part in the Sacred Cypher at GON, which is a dance event with a DJ and traditional pow wow group. Indigenous b-boys meld genres and dance as well. Creeazn was inspired by the energy and welcome that he received from XFRX in this event and he brought that spirit back with him and began to improve his skills and set up cypher circles in Edmonton, the most current of which is CypherWild.

Creeazn Today

Creeazn is now a teacher at the Boyle Street Education Centre, teaching Edmonton's inner-city youth how to develop their musical craft. He hosts traditional dance workshops and is always looking for more venues in which to host cyphers. He is also a club DJ and provides music complete with live cuts and scratches for the CypherWild block parties. He has plans to continue CypherWild, with consistent support from the Edmonton Arts Council. He also performs every year at the Edmonton Street Performer's Festival (SPF), most recently with his dance crew "Rhythm Speaks." At Edmonton SPF, his crew blends traditional and hip hop dance. There is a story telling aspect to their show through dance and language. These stories promote unity and encourage the audience to think in ways that overcome race, class, and religious segregation and to promote a healthier more vibrant and creative community. Creeazn exemplifies the values and practice of a firekeeper. It is in the fusion of Cree traditional practice and hip hop that CypherWild has power to change lives and move people, young and old, toward a greater appreciation for their community and themselves, wherever they are from.

Getting Involved

Creeazn can be contacted through the CypherWild YEG Facebook page (see Quick Links below). He may offer advice on how you can start similar cyphers in your community. Remember, everyone in the world is indigenous to somewhere and it's all about keeping the circle strong. Keep in mind that Creeazn's activism is about making local connections through an artistic lifestyle. Use your inspiration from reading his story to craft your own community activism.

Quick Links

- Boyle Street Education Centre: http://www.bsec.ab.ca
- CypherWild Facebook page: https://www.facebook.com/pages/CypherWild-YEG/123902341091949
- Gathering of Nations: http://www.gatheringofnations.com
- Truth and Reconciliation Commission of Canada: http://www.trc.ca
- The XFRX: http://www.thexfrx.com/#!pole_parties/c1h6a

Diana Pearson, Vancouver Island University, Edmonton, Alberta, Canada

Shima Robinson, MacEwan University, Edmonton, Alberta, Canada

Part 2

Youth Voices

Chapter 15

Notes on Part 2

Michael Holden

Over two years ago, our inaugural Youth Forum was hosted, gathering youth and their allies to identify challenges that concern youth, and to transform their social impact ideas into actionable projects. Throughout the following year, these youth activists worked extensively within their schools and with the local community to create meaningful change. These change initiatives took many forms, reflective of each group's passions and the needs they identified in their communities. Initiatives focused on mental health, Indigenous ways of knowing, creating community culture, homelessness, and social justice. Some groups addressed change within their schools, while others reached out to their neighborhoods and city-wide organizations. With the initiative by the Werklund School of Education, we have continued to host the Youth Forum twice a year.

In April 2017, participating youth were invited to document their process and share their experiences with other activists. This chapter is the culmination of that work. Students in grades 9 through 12, as well as their teachers, have contributed many of the contributions that follow. These pieces explore four key themes: the roles teachers and students found for themselves during the year, the process of creating change, the impact this work had on the youth and their communities, including the calls to action they have issued for other youth. We are indebted to the 37 students and teachers who have contributed to this book, as well as the many delegates who participated in each Forum. We admire their passion for change, their willingness to collaborate, and their ability to reflect and work to overcome barriers. They have created meaningful change for themselves and others that we are happy to share with you, our readers.

Michael Holden, Werklund School of Education, University of Calgary, Calgary, Alberta, Canada

Chapter 16

Occasion for Hope

Sharon Friesen

Youth are central to any conversation that involves them. They are the ones who can mobilize and make change in their schools and their community. However, they are kept out of adults' attempts to change programs, schools, or communities far too often. One of the commonplaces in education is that schools are about preparing youth for the future. Thought of this way, the entire endeavor becomes a kind of fortune-telling in which anyone's guess is as good as any other's. If the past is any indication, everybody's predictions are likely to be dead wrong. A student in the Werklund School of Education's Youth Forum put it this way, "schools are places we live our lives, not prepare for them."

There is a much more radical—and practical—approach to meeting youth where they are at today. Look closely at what the world is like *today*. What needs to be changed in today's schools to connect youth with the world they live in right now in meaningful ways?

To challenge taken-for-granted commonplaces in education, youth need to be included—in fact brought front and center in real ways as active agents of social change in their schools and communities, rather than viewed and treated as passive recipients. Indeed, schools *are* places where youth live their lives. Along with that living come issues, problems, and challenges that impact them. When youth are invited to come together to articulate these challenges, propose solutions and transform their social impact ideas into actionable projects, they build not only agency, but commitment and confidence to affect change. When youth mobilize to take action at the local level, in schools and in their communities, they come to know each other and the world through the real work that engages their minds, hearts, and spirits. Providing opportunities and supporting youth to engage in real work, work that makes a difference to them and their world, to come together to learn and share strategies for success is vital for all leaders, including youth leaders.

The Youth Forum at the Werklund School of Education was created to provide school-aged youth with an opportunity to come together; name their issues, problems and challenges; formulate possible solutions; and design a plan of action that they take back to their school. A teacher willing to provide support to the youth is also invited to attend the Youth Forum. The teacher is asked to listen. Undergraduate students facilitate conversations and work with each of the various youth groups.

Looking forward to what it would take for each of the students to carry through with their various action projects, they identified the following: determination, courage, the ability to consider diverse social perspectives; commitment to the change they were seeking to enact; willingness to follow through with their goals; a readiness to "fight to be given time and resources to pursue the issues" they identified; and willing to "go to places where their voice makes an impact." In coming together, the youth came to know each other and the world through work that engaged their minds and fueled their passion.

To get them started, the Werklund School provided each of the participating schools with funds to help launch their social action projects and a director of the Youth Forum stayed in contact with the teacher and youth in the schools, providing additional support as requested.

Now in its second year, the number of schools participating in the Youth Forum has doubled. Perhaps more importantly, the youth that participate in the forum are small in number compared to the number of youth these young people have mobilized in their respective schools. In one of the schools, youth formed a CCC Club (compassion, connection, and community) that are more than 200 strong. These students work actively to ensure students within the school are connected, and that their school is a place where everyone belongs. They also connect with their community, providing peer mentoring in the junior high and middle schools that are the feeder schools to their high school, making sandwiches for the homeless drop-in center, making craft kits for YWCA children and families affected by domestic violence, and reaching out to newly arrived immigrant and refugee youth across the city. In another school, youth working with school guidance counselors, community members, and Elders-in-Residence created a cultural wellness room to begin addressing mental health challenges in their school. They are also working to tackle climate change at the local level conducting an energy assessment, creating an art project, and placing solar panels on the horse barn on the school grounds. These are two out of the twenty schools in which youth have mobilized to make a positive and powerful difference in their schools and communities.

In addition to providing opportunities for the youth of the Youth Forum to come together, to take action, Dr. Shirley Steinberg created a place which honors not only the work of these youth, but also their voices. She invited the youth to give narrative form to their ideas and actions, and to give them voice to a wider audience. This book is a testament to her commitment to be involved, stay involved, and be the agent for change that the youth of our world needs.

Sharon Friesen, Professor, Werklund School of Education, University of Calgary, Calgary, Alberta, Canada

Chapter 17

Ten Hearts, One Thought

The Rant and Relate Team

Asbah, Shivom, Simerta, Reeana, Sanjeevani, Sadia, Divjot, Puneet, & Avreet

There were six of us. We were all basically strangers who never spoke more than a few words to each other. We came together because of one simple idea: the passion and desire to spread awareness around mental health and to break the stigmas surrounding it. However, this is wasn't how we started.

Originally, we were a group devoted to running our very own school blood drive. With Halloween just around the corner, we wanted to have both a food and blood drive, along with a haunted house at our school. We had done extensive research and we were super excited about this idea. However, we realized we weren't old enough to donate blood. We were very saddened by this, but we knew there were other obstacles we had to conquer as well. After traveling to the University of Calgary Youth Forum, we realized that there were many flaws in our original idea and the conversations at the university steered us in a different direction. We realized that all our passions weren't represented in our original initiative; we needed something we could all connect with. So, we pivoted!

Supporting Teacher Note (Ms. Gillis): Early in the term we had extensive conversation about the importance of identifying our passions to help motivate us to create meaningful change. The class was asked to design and implement an initiative that would have a positive impact on their community. It wasn't until their experience at the University of Calgary where they participated in a structured activity that got them thinking about the needs of youth today that they were provoked to think about wellness—and specifi-cally—mental health and wellness.

At the Youth Forum on we were asked three main guiding questions:

1. What are issues that youth face today?

2. What can we do about it?

3. What is our action plan?

These led us to brainstorm some key problems we see in our society. Some of the biggest issues that we came across were shifts of power, discrimination, and mental health illnesses. Shifts of power may include bullying, gender in-equality and a school environment where a teacher takes advantage of their position of power over a student; they may also occur in a work environment where there are higher and lower statuses leading to unfair differences and judgments. Discrimination may occur in areas of religion, race, mental health stigmas, or the LGBTQ+ community. Mental health illnesses may include suicide, isolation, depression, a poor quality of life, obsessive-compulsive dis-order, fear, anxiety, drug abuse, and so on. We learned that being a youth in this generation is very difficult. Many issues plague us such as technology and social media, social and emotional instability, family and background challenges, lack of appropriate role models and/or mentors, peer pressure, and simply just trying to figure out who we are as human beings and the roles we hope to play in society. After outlining the challenges, we began to think about what we could do and how we could take action. We really wanted our action plan to be a solution to ALL of these challenges.

After considering all of the issues that today's youth face, we began to think about our education system. Youth spend a majority of their time at school where they learn more than just the curriculum, but also how to in-teract socially by observing their peers and teachers. They are quite literally "growing up" at school. They are constantly being influenced by everything they observe and internalize. We began to research documents and curricu-lums to find ways to embed awareness and prevention of these issues in our everyday classes. We had many charts and lists of what education provided for us and what youth needed based on discussions at the university. We identi-fied the aspects in our learning that we were getting and those we were lack-ing. The comparison led us to think about how so many of our unaddressed needs can fit into health, wellness, and physical education classes. We came to the realization that mental health recurred throughout multiple health curric-ulums, yet it was rarely talked about or was just briefly touched on, often not to the point where it truly impacted students, challenged their thinking, or caused them to shift their way of living.

We were surprised by this and wanted to change the status quo, so we began to work for it. We set up multiple meetings with multiple teachers, to see if they would include these concepts in their lesson plans. We wanted to gather information to see if they also felt that these topics were important. In the beginning, our main goal was to seek constructive criticism and gain support without insulting the practice of teachers and/or staff. There were many ups and downs that came along with this process. Through seeking constructive criticism and support, we found teachers who also shared our passion for this issue. At times we felt discouraged and fired up because while teachers agreed with us on the importance of mental health awareness, they did not necessarily feel they could adjust their teaching styles to accommodate some of our suggestions. We realized many people aren't really open to change, even if they know it's for the better. Some teachers were willing to work with us, and without their support we couldn't have achieved anything.

Throughout the many meetings, we realized that we can impact students in multiple ways. This was inspiring because we the students were beginning to have a direct say in our learning. After our meetings with teachers, we decided it wasn't quite enough. We weren't creating a movement by changing classroom practices. We knew we had to do something else and something different. In time, we realized that the solution to the issues that we had been discussing required open, ongoing communication and empathy. So we created a place where we could do just that, which is how the Rant and Relate Team was born.

The Rant and Relate Team was created one day when we were all sitting together in our leadership class talking about our lives and, more specifically, our dilemmas. Somehow this time it went further and deeper than it had before; we opened ourselves up to one another and because of this, got to go beyond surface-level knowledge and actually form deeper connections. We were all able to empathize with the challenges each student was facing, proving that none of us were alone; we all felt so much better. If you were to walk into that class, it may have looked like we were totally off track, but in reality, we learned an important lesson: in order to experience a true sense of well-being, we need safe places where we can openly and honestly communicate and where we know we are being heard by people who can empathize and care. We wanted to get more people doing exactly what we had just done. We wanted to get more people talking about their challenges, challenges that are normally "uncomfortable" to talk about, but so very important. This is the world we live in. These are our lives. We need to start the conversation. We must care. For these reasons and many more, we began the Rant and Relate Team.

The title has a lot more meaning than you may think. To rant is to passionately express yourself, also to just let off steam when necessary. To relate is to find others that think alike and feel alike, it is to show that we aren't really all that different in the end. Our main motives were to build trust among ourselves, relieve stress and anxiety through talking to one another, build community, build a better understanding and sense of everyone that comes to the club, and finally, if someone is having a bad day, we believe we have the power inside of each of us to make it a little bit better for them. The club is a drop-in space for students in grades 5–9 to come together and connect once per week. We talk about good things, horrible things, passions, whatever we please, as it is completely student driven, but teacher supervised. We performed mindfulness, a practice that allows one to be at peace with themselves. We also did talking circles; with the talking bits becoming a quick Rant and Relate favorite. Not only have we seen grades integrating in a positive setting, students offering advice and moral support, but we also got to witness how each student lets off steam and how they provide support and help to others when it was their turn. We are huge believers in speaking on personal perspectives and experiences and not judging others, therefore we always made sure that students kept the names of people they were including in their 'rants' anonymous. We also believed in learning from our mistakes and accepting everyone for who they are. Teachers were also welcome to participate as equals to the students, which allowed us to build a sense of community and belonging, by connecting many diverse people through the sharing of ideas and opinions. It is a safe space where no one is denied and all thoughts are listened to and accepted.

From the creation of our Rant and Relate Club, our team and work has grown immensely! We partnered with the physical education team at our school to come up with and start Fun Fit Friday. Every Friday morning, students had access to an open gym space to come and play fun sports, games and activities. This was to show that physical health and well-being contributes to how we feel and to our mental health. It's super important to be healthy, but that can be fun too! Also, what better way is there to start off your morning than playing fun sports and activities? This allowed students to interact with other students from different grades and make new friends, which helped in building community.

Supporting Teacher Note: The Rant and Relate Team has played an integral part in getting Fun Fit Fridays off the ground. The program has had great success, and is heavily supported by the P.E. department as well as the Rant and Relate Team. The work these students have done is remarkable. Through all of their work they continually spoke with people to gather feedback, to inform any adjustments they made to their plans.

After listening to each other and communicating our thoughts and ideas clearly, we compromised and were able to come to agreements. We always tried our best to support each other, but we all have different ideas and beliefs, so discussions would get heated sometimes. We didn't agree on everything, but with every discussion we made sure we kept everyone's best interest in mind. Ultimately, we all had the same desire, which was to break stigmas, spread awareness, and start conversations. This passion is what connected us. When we made any decision, we made sure that it didn't go against our team moral and belief system, which we created in unison. We have learned that we can't let our differences and disagreements get to us—we must use them to improve and be better. We think mentors are very important as well, however, because what we do is so student-driven, they must know when to draw the line between when they should step in and when they should just let us figure it out and make mistakes and learn. Much of the growth we experienced came from us having to work things out ourselves. A mentor was present to guide the process and help us reflect, however, the majority of the legwork was done by us, which is what led to our personal growth. The way we improved was by receiving and applying feedback provided from the people we were trying to target with our work. Leading in this way was very new to us, and at first it was tedious for us to continuously go back and refine and polish our work. As time progressed we realized that it was only for the better, and the more we did it, the more innovative our ideas become. We always took time to reflect upon things that didn't work well or ideas people didn't like so that we could better address the needs of our audience. We used the "Design Thinking Process": Empathize, define, ideate, prototype, test, implement. Go back and do it all over again, and again, and again.

Supporting Teacher Note: As the students describe, they ran into challenges within their small group, as well as with peers from outside of the core Rant and Relate Team who did not necessarily take their work seriously. Most times students were able to work things out themselves.

We also thought that our experiences might connect to those with mental health issues, as they are needing to persevere and adjust in response to social stereotypes. Sometimes people say that they should go through it on their own, or they're "too sensitive" and "overreacting." What many don't seem to understand is that just because we can't see it, that doesn't mean it's not there. Take someone with cancer for example, would you ever tell them to fight it on their own? No. Mental pain and illness is just as bad as any physical pain. Not everyone is educated and aware of all of the issues people silently face, but that doesn't mean the problems aren't real. The hope is that those who are struggling are also learning how to be resilient, how to be strong, how to fight and persevere through life's battles: fall down, scrape your knees, get back up and repeat. We have learned this through our own experiences with Rant and Relate. There were days where we were just lost and we didn't know what to do or where to go. At these times we had a strong support system of teachers and friends that gave us constant inspiration, motivation, and support. Without them, we wouldn't have been able to keep going forward. Now we want to pay it forward and be that support system for someone in a similar situation; we want to create a change that would allow students at our school to be the reason one of their peers received hope in a hard time. It is very important to have someone by your side, during these times. These are the times where you grow most as an individual, and it's important for people to know that they aren't alone.

Despite our successes within the club, we still felt like we needed to reach more of our school population; we wanted to go school-wide! We came up with a few ideas, which eventually evolved into our First Annual Mental Health Awareness Event and we chose May 3, 2017 for the event, as it was "Hats On For Mental Health Day." Our school had taken up Hats On the previous year, but there was little conversation about mental health at that time, meaning that awareness of mental health issues or the stigmas surrounding them weren't really addressed. It was more about fundraising, with students and staff paying two dollars to wear their hat for the day. In fact, many did not know what mental health illness or stigmas even meant, so our goal was to make sure that by the end of this year they did and they had solutions on how we could prevent it.

We began the conversation before the event, debriefing afterwards, and following up with action plans in the weeks after it had ended. We wanted to make sure everyone had the chance to change the way they thought about mental illness. We asked each student to approach the day with an open mind and heart and to listen to the speakers and really consider what they had to say. Our hope was that students would participate in the lessons, reflect on the messages, and know that each of us is aiming for similar things: to connect, to feel valued, to feel well.

The day began with students in their mixed homerooms. A mixed homeroom is when students from grade 5, 6, 7, 8 and 9 are mixed up together to form one class. When mixed homeroom groups had assembled with their teachers in various spaces throughout the school, the students were handed yellow bracelets and asked to write a label that either society gives them or that they give themselves. This was inspired by the "Wear Your Label Campaign" and allowed students to become vulnerable by opening up about themselves in hopes they could trust and participate in the conversations that arose throughout the day. Our mental health is a serious thing. We warned students that the day may make some a bit anxious as it required them to let their guards down and take their masks off. We encouraged students with the message that "it's okay to not be okay sometimes." We all have stories to share. What has happened to you, how you feel, what you're thinking, are all parts of who you are and they're important.

Our entire school then participated in an assembly with two keynote speakers. The first speaker was from the Canadian Mental Health Association and spoke about mental health and illness, stigma, recovery and getting help. The second keynote address was from EmpowerMind, and helped us understand our potential for individual growth by participating in mindfulness and yoga activities. Our assembly was designed to be a powerful start to the day that would cause a shift in thinking. The students then participated in two breakout sessions during the rest of the morning, the majority being expert sessions run by various organizations from throughout the city, and a few student-developed and -driven sessions. The unique part of our event was the fact that we created lessons that were delivered to students by students. We made sure that the lessons would be age-appropriate for all students in grades 5 through 9 and tried to keep our sessions as interactive and conversational as possible. Our main objective was to have students empathize with one another and for them to relate to us and one another. We felt that the message coming from us rather than teachers would be significantly more impactful. Some themes from the day included: self-expression, mindfulness, yoga, reflection, the power of our words, resiliency, self-image, finding and giving hope, stress management, and many more. Sessions that were not led by students were led by experts in various fields, helping us gain insights and find solutions to our challenges.

After the sessions, we wanted students to have a reflection period. Each mixed homeroom debriefed and created a "Hope Tree." With this reflection,

our goal was to encourage students to think about their hopes for both themselves and their school community. The roots of the tree were words, such as
respect, equality and bully-free. These were values our students had brainstormed earlier in the year. The leaves were simple actions that the students
did to make change happen within our community. Some examples included: holding the door open, smiling to strangers, random acts of kindness,
not being a bystander, complimenting others, volunteering, picking up trash,
making people laugh, and so on. Students printed their actions on the leaves
and together built the tree.

Our team has faced many ups and many downs. It was hard for us to
come face to face with some of these challenges, but we persevered. One of
our treasured memories was the train ride to the University of Calgary. We
started the ride with awkward smiles and fake laughs being that we were just
acquaintances at the time. But after the conference, we opened up to each
other since we had found a topic to connect us. Each and every single one of
us took risks and just trusted each other. We became vulnerable. We shared
personal experiences and stories. We have cried together. We have laughed
together. We always found a way to figure things out. We are truly one of the
greatest teams of all time. Not only have we grown as a team, we have grown
as individuals. Every single person on the team has a purpose, a reason for
being there. Strengths are acknowledged, and we find inspiration in our own
lives. We aim to clearly communicate with one another and the work is genuinely 'fun' for us! We have a Rant and Relate group chat, allowing for ongoing
sharing of ideas. It also keeps all of us on track by helping us stay on the same
page. We have a calendar, sign-up sheets, and many, many to-do lists. On
Fridays, we have "download" sessions where we come together and share what
we have accomplished, what our goals are, and how we will achieve what is
remaining. We've gone from just being acquaintances to feeling like a family.

There is no purpose in making a change that isn't sustainable and long
lasting. The original six members of Rant and Relate are grade nine students.
We won't be at our current school next year as we are moving on to high
school. Due to this we are seeking out grade 5 to 8 students who share similar
passions as us. We are actively recruiting students from younger grades at our
school to keep the core beliefs and work of Rant and Relate alive. We have
been talking with students who have attended our club and believe in the
work that we do, students who share our passion for student wellness here at
Ted Harrison. We plan on workshopping students in younger grades to teach
them how to plan lessons and coordinate to achieve their goals. Our current
thinking is they will partner up with the Mixed Homeroom committee. Orig-

inally, we worked with the Mixed Homeroom committee to incorporate our follow-up lesson plans at a school-wide level so we could keep the change going. Now our hope is that, with teacher support, students can lead the work that takes place every week, and integrate some of the values and beliefs from Rant and Relate. We also hope to keep our school-wide event going as an annual event. We believe that Rant and Relate offers so many possibilities for students. We personally want to dispel the beliefs that the youth of today are powerless in the face of large societal issues. Take us for an example: we were provoked at a Youth Forum and from there, we the students took control in lobbying teachers to support our cause. We want passionate and motivated students like us to keep this going because we believe it is important. We are also working to make this club a possibility at the high schools we will be attending by seeking teacher buy-in and support.

Our journey doesn't end here. This is the beginning of a new legacy; it will carry on for our years to come. A huge thanks to the following:

- Ms. Gillis. She helped in making everything a possibility. Continuously guiding us, never rejecting our ideas...even if they were really, really weird. We would not have been able to accomplish this without her.

- Ted Harrison's student leaders and our leadership team, those in the official classes and those who have stepped up to help anyway.

- The Mixed Homeroom committee, for their feedback and willingness to work with us to continue the learning beyond our school-wide event and this school year.

- Administration, for the go-ahead and support in making Rant and Relate and our school-wide Mental Health Awareness Day a reality, and to all of the teachers and staff at Ted Harrison who are helping to support the learning that is taking place and will continue to take place.

- Ted Harrison students, for engaging in learning about mental health and wellness. This is a big topic, and we hope you took away at least one new understanding as you reflect on who you are and who you want to be. No movement is possible without a participating follower-ship!

- Everyone else that believed in us. Had hope in us. Pushed us forward. Gave us the required resources and skills to move forward and onwards.

- And finally, a huge thank you to the Youth Forum. With your provocation and financial support, we were able to create a change that we hope has affected lives.

Thank you.
With love and compassion, <3
The (ever-growing) Rant and Relate Team

Asbah, Shivom, Simerta, Reeana, Sanjeevani, Sadia, Divjot, Puneet & Avreet with Eleanor Gillis, Ted Harrison School, Calgary, Alberta, Canada

Chapter 18

Brunch Buddies

A Time for Students to Build Positive Cross-grade Relationships

Bridgette, Ian, McKinley, Owen, Angela, Ethan, Michelle, & Peyton

Our names are: Bridgette, Ian, McKinley, Owen, Angela, Ethan, Michelle and Peyton, we are grade nine students at Arbour Lake Middle School. We may not be the most popular, academic, or athletic students, but we have created a legacy.

After attending a youth leadership symposium, we were left to ponder the question each and every student at the event was asked: "What issues are youth faced with today?"

Following a lot of discussion we molded an idea around our answers to this question, which encompassed the need for more face-to-face conversations, nutrition and mental well-being. As we are graduating this year and our mentor teachers educate the youngest grades in the school we consistently reflected upon our memories:

- "I remember when I first came to this school. I thought it was so big!"
- "I remember walking through the hallways with my elbows out..."
- "I still walk with my elbows out! It's the only way to get where you need to be!"
- "Grade nine's always seemed so scary to me, but we're not!"
- "Life was so much easier back then."

If only we knew then what we know now.

With these recollections, we came upon our idea to talk with and mentor younger students in our school. We wanted to debunk the myth that grade nines are scary, and share our experiences and tips with the naive younger students in our school. Our Friday schedule allowed time once a month for us to provide nutrition in the form of juice and muffins and some honest conversations with a group of younger students. And so came the Breakfast (later to be Brunch) Buddies.

Our conversations always began with the same question: What issues are youth faced with today? And it seemed that every grade had its issues, or lack thereof: The fifth graders seemed to be comfortable in a new school and overly-focused on the muffins and scrap paper to draw on. The seventh graders felt that they were finally fitting in. They were catching up with the pace of middle school, and actually helped us clean up at the end of the brunch. The sixth graders, it seemed, were dealing with the most stress. With Provincial Achievement Exams on the horizon, a lot of them were worried about what this test would be like and how it would affect their "permanent records." Things like friendships, locker troubles and the increasing amount of homework worried them. These students were not afraid of us, and were happy to accept our "been there done that" stories of experience. We provided relief in our attesting to survive the turmoil of middle school.

Brunch Buddies quickly became known around the school, and soon students would ask when it would be their turn for juice and muffins with the grade nines. We are happy to have made a difference by creating a strengthened cross-grade community within our school. Brunch Buddies will live on as eight grade-eight (soon to be grade-nine) students will be trained to be the next Bridgette, Ian, McKinley, Owen, Angela, Ethan, Michelle and Peyton. Our legacy of providing comfort and peace of mind is important to us and we are happy to see what has become of the Brunch Buddies.

A Note from Three Teachers

From a teacher's perspective, it was interesting to watch students from different grades interact with one another during such a casual encounter. We were happy to negotiate times and provide a safe and supervised environment for the Brunch Buddies meet-ups to occur. We couldn't be more proud of these strong individuals for starting and leaving their legacy. Brunch Buddies encompasses the social beings that these eight individuals (and students in general) are. It was really nice to see and hear our younger students leave Brunch Buddies with smiles on their faces and pleas of another try. What this initiative has proven is that students crave conversation. It is time to put the phones down, and indulge in the art of full-fledged conversation.

Brunch Buddies: A Poem
by Megan Krzyżańska

We are teenagers.
We are misunderstood.
We aren't always given opportunities,

But give us a question and some freedom
and we might surprise you.

At a youth leadership symposium
we were given a question:
What issues are youth faced with today?

Technology.
Too much of it, and not enough
    Face -- to -- Face
conversations.

We are in the 9th grade.
Kings and Queens of middle school.
The younger students avoid our hallways
because we are "scary and mean."
They don't really know us.

Health encompasses nutrition and mental
wellbeing.
With a need for conversation and health,
we brainstormed our initiative
and we asked the kids:

What issues are youth faced with today?

Technology.
Bullies.
Crowded Hallways.
Provincial Achievement Exams.
Friendships.
The list goes on...

And the Breakfast Buddies was born
(Due to scheduling, schooling and release
from our teachers
The name was changed to Brunch
Buddies).
A place for younger students to sit 3 at a
table with
a grade 9 leader.

A safe place where their voices of concern
are shared with a trusted youth.
We alleviate stress,
debunk rumors,
and create lasting cross-grade relationships
with our young participants.

We teach them the "tricks of the trade,"
while enjoying muffins and juice
because not everybody comes to school
with a full belly.

This is our legacy.
something that will live on
long after we graduate.
But we pioneered it.
We made a difference
because we were given the opportunity
to help in a way that we knew we could...
With some juice, muffins
and a little bit of conversation.
We are the Brunch Buddies. :)

Bridgette, Ian, McKinley, Owen, Angela, Ethan, Michelle, Peyton, Megan Krzyżańska, Arbour Lake School, Calgary, Alberta, Canada

Chapter 19

Nelson Mandela High School and the #MandelaCares Project

Laiba, Mariam, Hadia, Mansi, Jenny, Ms. Martin, Mr. Chee, & Mr. Sagriotis

O ften, we are told of the stories of success and about how one person is capable of immense powers—powers that can possibly change the world for the better, or for the worst. As the youth, and the future of our nations and societies, we are told to be emboldened by the positive stories, and to move forward in this world to create our own impact. So, we turn towards those who have paved the path for the greater good—we turn to the heroes of our societies, and with our tiny, impressionable selves, we attempt to walk in their footsteps.

Nelson Mandela, Martin Luther King, Barack Obama, Malala Yousafzai; all of them are notable people, who started with a small story, and worked on turning that into a legacy. Their legacies carried on, their positive impact weaving through the fabrics of society, creating patterns of change and leaving behind peace, and unity. As the ribbon of change passes by us, we, the youth, attempt to clutch it and ask ourselves, 'How can I create positive change?' It's hard to do, especially when we don't understand who we are, and what we are capable of.

In 2016, Nelson Mandela High School opened its doors to students for the first time. As the students poured in, they also brought with them their dreams and desires. In order to accommodate all these beliefs, our staff strived to give us the tools we needed to be successful. However, along with tools, we also needed some very vital changes in our school. That is where the youth came in.

In September, student delegates came together to discuss what issues our students may be facing. We determined that some of the largest issues often impacting and hindering students from accomplishing their dreams were often the environment of the school. It's hard to allow your creativity to grow when you are surrounded by negativity. It's even harder when you're an immigrant, and have to deal with both the cultures of the society you live in and the society you (or your parents) were initially from. Thus, Nelson Mandela High School is initiating a year-long project that will focus on positive inclusivity, creating a better environment, and establishing a school spirit and 'culture'.

Our project will begin in the second year of our school, when we will be welcoming hundreds of more students (boosting our population to 1,800). Along with new students, our school will also be opening its doors to grade 12 students. With our population and enrollment levels at an all-time high, we hope to initiate the first phase of our project and complete all three phases by the end of the year.

As we have mentioned, our project has three phases. The first phase will be a banner and a pledge that we have created. As Nelson Mandela starts its official second year, our group has decided that we want all of our fellow students to know that they belong in a safe and welcoming community by reminding them of the responsibilities we all share to ensure the wellbeing of this school community. Thus, we have devised a pledge we hope our students will say in the school's opening ceremony:

> I pledge to create a safe, warm, and welcoming environment in my school community. I pledge to be an ambassador and acceptor of change and hope. I pledge to embrace equality, diversity, and promote unity in our school. I pledge to value the diverse backgrounds, knowledge, and history that all individuals in this school bring every single day. I pledge to respect myself, my peers, and my superiors. I pledge to take care of my school environment, and help maintain a safe facility for all students to use. As a citizen of this school, I hereby promise to continuously follow these words, and advocate for them not only in school, but in my personal life as well.

This pledge was created based off of feedback we received from our student advisory group about what Mandela's society should be like. We hope that by taking this pledge, the students at Mandela promise to follow these values and uphold a positive community. Furthermore, after taking this pledge, we will have a banner with Nelson Mandela High School's official logo, and a picture of Mr. Mandela himself, for students to sign their names. By signing their names, students are further promising to uphold the values of the pledge, and are thus igniting their process of becoming part of the Nelson Mandela school community.

Our second phase is creating a room that will be designated for meetings where students are free to share their feelings, and are free to express themselves and any concerns they may have. We are looking forward to finding a teacher who can act as an adult chaperone for the room. We are hoping that this 'safe' room will be student-led, and it can be a method for students to relieve themselves of their worries and problems by leaning on peers for help and support.

Our final phase is the community mural art. Our previous phases were designed for the student body, in order to establish a feeling and culture of belonging and comfort; these phases dealt with improving and attending to the mental and spiritual needs of our students as well as the formation of our school's culture. As our students begin to feel more welcome in our school society, and more comfortable with expressing themselves without having to fear judgment, we want to hone their individual skills and create a community mural that will be the physical embodiment of the school's positive environment. We are currently working with Mr. Mikhail Miller, our school's artist in residence, and our principal, Ms. Martin, in getting a school mural approved. Since this will be a community mural, we're hoping to get student input regarding all phases of the mural art (themes of each artwork, colors, and so on).

Our school is divided into various communities within each grade (for example, all grades have -four communities—A, B, C, D—which meet up once a week for a period of time to further develop school community and unity). Thus, we will use these communities to our benefit, and will give each community one large board for each student to design art. Since our school will have a multitude of students, we have chosen to give them the overall theme of, "Mandela Speaks: What does Nelson Mandela High School Have to Say?" The communities will use this overall theme to design what topic they would like to express (for example, perhaps one group would like to talk about the diversity at our school), and they will have the freedom to draw or paint their designs.

We hope that our project is able to empower our fellow peers and build connections with them; allowing them to resolve their own issues, as well as provide helpful solutions to others who may face the same ones. In a world of negativity, divided by hatred towards others' differences, we want our students to feel they matter and are being heard, and make them feel comfortable in reaching out for guidance from their fellow peers to achieve their goals. By coming together in unity to find strong solutions for problems we all face around the world, they will also have the necessary tools to make change, and this can motivate the students to take on active roles in their school community and other communities as well. This is how Nelson Mandela High School plans on creating, and leaving behind, a positive legacy in our world. We hope we have inspired others to also grab onto the ribbon of change, and continue to weave their own positive impact in our societies; now, and onwards.

#MandelaCares project, Laiba, Mariam, Mansi, Jenny, Ms. Martin, Mr. Chee, Mr. Sagriotis, Nelson Mandela High School, Calgary, Alberta, Canada

Chapter 20

The Future Will Be Found in Walking Together

Sameer Harris & Alix Esterhuizen

When we map the course of history in broad strokes, we see the progressive movement towards human rights, equality, and the ideals of liberalism, a constant march to alleviate the struggles of others when possible, and in doing so creating an open, free, and multicultural world. Our predecessors, our parents and grandparents, dreamed of this world, and saw the promotion of activism as the fundamental route to ensure the rights of individuals, regardless of country of origin. This is the world that we were fortunate enough to inherit.

However, we are currently bearing witness to the rise of populist forces who advocate for personal advancement and the condemnation of anything new or unknown. Our world is becoming increasingly antagonistic to the plight of the misfortune-d and desperate. This political climate has seen the rise of cynicism, apathy, and the degradation of humanist ideals, a climate which seemingly is pushing back the hands of time. This culture is not only pervasive in our politics, but is unfortunately influencing the way we treat other people and the community around us. In a world currently marred by conflict and poverty, this divisive and selfish rhetoric cannot help solve our problems, as they only seek to divide us, not unite us.

Our world cannot sustain this selfish thinking. Now, more than ever, is the time to embrace and appreciate others. We need to reinvigorate our desire for activism, as activism is the key to making the world a better place. However, the media we consume presents us with two versions of activism. The first involves a celebrity face, the kind of activism that results in a handshake over a comically large check. The second involves protest signs, often ending in tear gas and clashes with police in riot gear. These two visions of activism are constantly imposed on us, and we are given the impression that anything less does not and cannot count.

We wholeheartedly propose abandoning these narrow visions of activism. These are not the kinds of activism we need right now. We wish to instead propose our vision of activism, the kind of activism we believe our future requires.

In 2015, the Truth and Reconciliation Commission of Canada published their Calls to Action, to "redress the legacy of residential schools and advance the process of Canadian reconciliation" (p. 1). The process of reconciliation may be the most important endeavor of our generation, and it will not be an easy one. This process, though, encapsulates what our activism needs to be.

As part of our multiculturalism week, we held a school-wide poster design competition for the phrase "We Are All Treaty People;" the winning designs were framed and placed in our main office. Shortly after the posters were mounted, our school held one of its in-school blood drives. In the course of conversation with some of the individuals in our school running the blood drive, the posters came up—they had noted them in the office while signing in, but did not know what was meant by "treaty people." Despite having lived in Calgary, they had no idea that we live on Treaty 7 land. This Treaty, signed in 1877, provided the official exchange of land between the Blackfoot Nations, including the Siksika, the Piikani, and the Kainai, and the Canadian federal government.

By most of the metrics that we define success by, that interaction was insignificant. However, it exemplifies what we believe activism to be. Canadian philosopher John Ralston Saul argues that Canadian multiculturalism is distinct. We still embrace the concept, and have not been lost in anti-immigration rhetoric and ethnic nationalism. We are an anomaly. What makes our multiculturalism work is found in the root of what Canada is; a country built out of a long relationship with Indigenous peoples and their "philosophies of inclusion," one founded in "between the place, the group and the individual" (2016). Canadian multiculturalism works because we continually ask why it works, because we continually return to it as a concept and never cease to talk about it. This, too, is what we feel activism needs to be a continued conversation, the sum of small actions and ideas.

This cannot be a novel vision of activism, but it is one we do not hear enough. So while we have no succinct summary of our idea of what activism ought to be, we want to reiterate the rough edges of its outline, to emphasize what we feel activism and conscious choice in our actions can accomplish. Activism is not something you engage in alone. It is something you participate in with others—the small actions you each take collectively add up to something more. Activism lives, not in grand gestures, but in conversations, chance encounters, and the moments we can cultivate through our care and consideration. Collectively we make a difference, and that is how we know our future will be found in walking together.

References

Ralston Saul, J. (2016). Canada's multiculturalism: A circle, ever edging outwards. The Globe and Mail. Retrieved from: https://www.theglobeandmail.com/news/national/canadas-multiculturalism-a-circle-ever-edging-outwards/article29719178/

Truth and Reconciliation Commission of Canada. (2015). Truth and Reconciliation Commission of Canada: Calls to Action. Retrieved from: http://www.trc.ca/websites/trcinstitution/File/2015/Findings/Calls_to_Action_English2.pdf

Sameer Harris & Alix Esterhuizen, Centennial High School, Calgary, Alberta, Canada

Chapter 21

It

Maxwell Starko

Dedicated to the dear, beautiful hearts of CCC. May this club give you the perspective and the escapism you need.

In the morning there was something different, its usual cool guarded demeanor was off, and it sat there silently waking up, leaving me to bask in its energy. Its left eye was slightly more shut than the other, and it hated this. It was small, not in a legal little person way, but in a comfortable average height of 5'9. It was one year older, and it never failed to remind me. We would always go to the top of this parking garage in Kensington and it would scream when I hoisted myself up on the edge, afraid of me falling. I would sit there because the wind was warm and it and I had the perfect shot of the whole word. As the golden rays lifted up its bleached hair, its eyes shut, intent on soaking up every moment. When it talked things were different, I swear it said my name differently than others, like it knew something about me others didn't. Band tees were its specialty, it rocked them everywhere until it became cold. After that, they were quickly replaced with jeans and letterman jackets. It was a terrific singer and always wanted to sing something it hadn't before. It wanted music to be authentic. It wanted to be authentic. There was something about its "adolescent rebel" vibrations that were contagious, and when we were together something in me was warm. We argued endlessly about the void of space above us, and how small we really were. We argued until we finally decided we both had no idea what was happening up there and fell into each other's arms, a feeling of safety and eternal comfort. Then it told me "A comfort zone is a beautiful place, but nothing ever grows there." I didn't understand it. For months, it would call me "sweetie" every time I saw it. Not in a motherly way, as it was not my mother, but in a mocking way. Mocking everyone around us who thought pet names for each other were endearing. We were too cool for that. It knew something everyone else didn't, I don't know what it was, but it did. Everything about it was magical. On a particularly warm September afternoon, we went to our usual spot—the parking garage seemed to mend all of our problems. Our eyes glued to the big blue sky, we were in a euphoric state. No pain, prejudice, anxiety, or colossal exam could take that away from us. It looked at me and said, "Let's give everyone a piece of this sky." I left, more confused than I had ever been in my life. A few months went by and as winter drew near our spot became less and less accessible. I began to think about how the spot made me feel, a vacation of sorts. My escape from an often painful reality.

Author's Note

Maxwell Starko is one of the student leaders of Compassion, Connection, and Community (CCC), a social activist group at Western Canada High School in Calgary, Alberta. CCC students engage in activities to build students' capacity for compassion and connection in their community. The students hope to build a lasting legacy of "paying it forward" at Western. They are committed to creating a culture of local community and social activism "simply because it is the right thing to do." As Maxwell explains, "CCC gives students an escape, a place to be heard and respected. Those who observe our world with empathy and compassion gravitate towards CCC. We work together to create change within our community. In return, we receive a purpose. Our perspectives shift and we allow ourselves to lead a meaningful life through our community work."

Maxwell Starko, Western Canada High School, Calgary, Alberta, Canada

Chapter 22

Dear People My Age

Andreea Alexandra Duica

Dear People My Age,

Sometimes the prospect of "making the world a better place" can seem like a bold challenge designed exclusively for individuals of great caliber. I know of many youth who consider this to be true. If you are one of them, please, for the sake of all things good, do not see that thought through to fruition. Rip it from your mind, crumple it up, and toss it in the waste bin, because that is where it belongs. Anyone, regardless their race, age, or physical ability has the capacity to make the world a better place. I know this because I have been doing it unconsciously for years. And it is likely that many of you stand in a similar position. If you intend to spend your life fighting for others or promoting an empowering message, then surprise! You are an activist in the making.

In the past, teens were often excluded from participation in social movements because it was always the adults who commanded the discourse. But this idea that youth possess little power to be vocal in society is one of the vilest myths out there. My friends, do not let anyone discredit your worth. If anything, our ability to perceive the world with a fresh set of eyes gives us a distinct advantage when it comes to identifying and eradicating issues. Though we may be young, we have also inherited the opportunity to push the world forward at an unimaginable rate. Take a look at me, for example.

An activist is a word that I never thought I would use to describe myself in a million years. Yet, here I am!

I'm certain my own journey began long before I could catalogue it in my brain, however I'd like to believe that the first moment I truly began to see myself as an activist was during a short presentation I gave with a fantastic group of girls in support of a local nonprofit organization. If my recollections serve me right, this took place at a local community center on a Friday night, and we had pulled up to the final slide on our Prezi. With our hearts full of the love and energy radiating from the crowd, we were relieved to be finished our last public speaking event of the year. But just as we were making our way off the stage, a kind woman approached my group. We were prepared to be showered with compliments, but to our surprise, she simply said, "Ladies, there was something about your presentation that bothered me immensely." My bloated heart shrunk by a factor of 10 as I processed those words. I pulled out my script, hunting desperately for any phrase that could have been remotely offensive. I found nothing. Perplexed by her comment, I shot her a confused look. The lady smiled and said, "You might be young, but do not degrade yourselves by saying that you have not yet begun to impact your world. Do not underestimate the power of your actions. Those small contributions are extremely valuable."

I took another look at the piece of paper in my hand. And it all clicked. I had written, "Even though we're young and we still have a long way to go before we truly begin to impact our world, we were still capable of spreading the word about this charity, and making a donation through the Youth Philanthropy Initiative that would ease the financial stress of at least three families." She never told me her name, that kind woman. But her words stick with me to this day. To many, those small philanthropic endeavors might seem extraordinary, but to me, at the time, they were not. As a result of that experience, I learned that the idea of "good activism" is not limited by one's ability to produce grand movements in a short span of time. And it does not always entail burning symbols of national pride because of the injustices the government imposes upon others. Good activism can be small gestures of kindness that, over time, combine to create incremental change.

Now, there are a number of narratives out in the world that disagree with this. And I'm not saying that they're completely blasphemous, but they are definitely misleading. I have watched multiple videos on YouTube presenting the argument that only offline activists who go out on the streets and protest are the "real" activists; that anything less is "slacktivism." This message is toxic, especially to individuals like us who can utilize social media to spread waves of positivity; it demeans anyone who is using their platform to raise awareness. Awareness in and of itself is a form of educating others. And education is activism in its most fundamental form. Even a gesture as plain as wearing a shirt that reads "The Future is Female," posting ideas on internet forums, signing petitions, striking out against injustice in the comment section of a video, or even sharing a J.K. Rowling tweet can make a significant difference. Instead of belittling the individual who does this and calling them a "slacktivist," be proactive and add to the conversation. Listen to their story and perhaps you'll learn something. Even better, there's a chance that those interactions will inspire you to take that message and develop it further. The idea of slacktivism is contrived, and a waste of brain space. Silence anyone who tells you otherwise, because all they serve to do is divide us as a broader movement. Do not let them win. Appreciate that different people will get involved in different ways. Use and celebrate that! If you possess the power to do something, anything (even if it's as small as holding a door open for someone) you should do it. And if an opportunity arises that enables you to do more, you should seize that, too.

One of the most profound issues with our generation nowadays is that we are presented with so many incredible opportunities to broaden our horizons, but instead of welcoming them, we often let them slip away. Why? Is it because we are unsure of where to start? Is it that we don't have time to put in the necessary effort? Or is it simply because of the convenience of concerning ourselves solely with our own personal problems? Perhaps it is a bit of all three. My point is that there will always be a force that attempts to erode your altruism. For me, that force was the very thing that brought me into this world: my parents.

Being born outside of Canada is not uncommon, nor is it a bad thing by any means, however it does play a significant role in shaping your global perspective. For reasons I could never fully discern, my Romanian parents were extremely conservative and anti-liberal; they always encouraged me to take care of myself first and foremost, instead of "burning out my efforts" to serve other people. My best guess is that they were simply raised to abandon any hope that the world still harbored people with good intentions, because our country was full of corruption. No Romanian political party, business, or nonprofit organization was without its fair share of exploitative strategies, so it would be disrespectful for me to scrutinize my parents for attempting to protect me. But despite my appreciation for their preemptive safety measures, I continued to go forward in pursuit of what I believed in. I have my educators to thank for that. Volunteering, presenting, going to conferences at the university, and taking part in school initiatives would not have crossed my mind if I hadn't had access to multiple viewpoints on the global spectrum. I might never have come across the practice of activism, nor would I have found a variety of mediums through which I could be my authentic self, were it not for my mentors who used their passion for teaching to guide me and my peers through the obstacles of life. I do not take any of them for granted, and I urge you to do the same. Tune out whatever is holding you back, no matter how blaring its noise may be. Instead, take the hands of those who support you, and step out of your confinements in unison.

Yet another issue I've noticed is that some teens have gotten a little lost in the idea of creating social change. This is because, in recent years, ideas of social consciousness and activism have been branded with the coveted "popular" label. I do admit, the fact that our meme-obsessed generation is managing to harbor such progressive trends in the midst of so much goofiness is incredibly promising, however, if you're someone who is deciding to participate in a movement for the sole purpose of conforming to a label, or using it as a means to boost your resume, then you should not be in it, period. Please do not misunderstand, I am not suggesting that you halt your mission altogether, because I'm sure many of us share an intrinsic desire to work for a cause bigger than ourselves. The only message I want to convey here is the importance of finding a cause you genuinely care about, and are willing to put in a lifetime worth of effort to uphold. Though, I admit the task of finding a cause is easier said than done. Especially when us teens are still in the process of finding ourselves. In a world that expels problem after problem at an exponential rate, it's become increasingly easier for all those possible causes to overwhelm us. This gives rise to complicated question like: Which problem do I tackle first? Am I limited to a single one? How do I even begin to find a solution to them all? They key, I've realized, is to absolve all of those mental weights. Begin by letting go; release all your fears about losing face by being vulnerable and real, because you have nothing to prove to anyone. And do not hunt for a problem to try and "care about;" because that will only lead to false conclusions. The key is to go out into the world with zero expectations and let the problems find you. Like I said, its overflowing with them. Whichever ones cling to your heart the strongest are the ones you should be pursuing with all your might.

At the end of the day, the magic of activism can be found within the actions and conversations that your discoveries fuel. So make a conscious effort to engage with others who have a message to share; ask them questions, open yourself up to learning, and immerse yourself in the vast community of thinkers, dreamers, and doers. Better yet, take the hand of your fellow activists and say "Hey, let's make the world a better place together."

One step, no matter its size, can make a tremendous difference as long as it is headed in the right direction. Remember this as you embark on your new journey as an activist.

With love,
Alex

Andreea Alexandra Duica, Centennial High School, Calgary, Alberta, Canada

Chapter 23

"We Have to Listen to Our Kids, and Understand Where They're Coming From"

Interview with Karsen Black Water & Shane Wells

Editor's Note:
The following is a transcript of a conversation between Karsen Blackwater, Shane Wells, Shirley Steinberg, and Michael Holden. Karsen, a student leader at Kainai High School, and Shane, one of the school's Guidance Counsellors, met with Shirley and Michael in November 2017 to share their experiences leading change with their school and their community. The conversation took place in the school's Cultural Wellness Room, which features a large teepee created by students, Kainai staff, and the school's Elders in Residence. Karsen and Shane reflect on their experiences with these initiatives, as well as their experiences living and working in an Indigenous community that continues to celebrate and build upon its traditions and identity. Their experiences with the Youth Forum are but one part of their ongoing efforts in addressing youth leadership, mental health, and climate change. We are grateful to Shane and Karsen for being so candid in their responses, and for sharing both the successes and challenges in their work.

Shane: Well, my kids aren't very social, and they don't really know how to explain things. They think the teacher might get offended, so it's just hard for a lot of kids to communicate and have a trusting relationship. I think building the bond will be a lot better for our schooling, and if kids feel more comfortable talking to their teachers and being more active in class, then the participation rates and attendance rates will skyrocket. I think, even for myself, it's kind of hard to talk to teachers; they can seem kind of daunting in a way. It's hard because there's always the judgment of having a younger mindset, [the teachers think]: "You don't understand what we're trying to discuss. You're just not mature enough."

I really think that brings down students' self-esteem, and so we want to find ways we could communicate better between students and teachers. That's why we came up with this suggestion box.

Shirley: Do you want to share how you came from an off-reserve school, and [what it was like to] come here?

Karsen: It's way different from my old school. I did see some similarities between students, because of the society nowadays. With teachers, I think more so off-reserve, they're not very [present] in the students' life. They're just there to teach, and that's all they are there for.

I remember my one teacher saying, "I'm not your babysitter. We're not here to look after you," and that kind of feels like there's a trust issue with them. But here, they're more active in our lives, especially in wanting to help you succeed.

Having things like being able to take part in different forums and speak out about things like this, I think that really builds a voice for students; especially me, coming from a school where I got told to not express what I was thinking. I was never given the chance to say what I thought.

I remember in a social studies class, my teacher was talking about our [Native] ways, and since I was one of the only Natives in that class, I tried to put in my input, and she'd say, "That's not right." Coming from a reserve where I grew up, and knowing about my own people, it was kind of a shock to me.

But here, we're all the same. We all have that understanding of where we come from, and learning about it, and it's just easier to accept who we are, and just be able to express our ideas.

Shirley: So, were you involved in [building the tipi]?

Karsen: Yeah. When we came back from the Youth Forum—I think both of them—we started thinking more about it and building on it. We came up with the idea of it, and brainstormed about it.

Shirley: Came up with the idea of what?

Karsen: Of this room, and we're usually coming up with different ways we could have students be more involved in the cultural aspect and perspective, and tying in regular Western ways to our traditional ways.

We wanted to bring in this room and have influence from our elders, so we have an Elders and Residents Program, and we actually met with the elders. Me and a couple of other students, we sat in this room, and nothing was in it—it was completely bare. We started coming up with ideas.

Shirley: You mean just with the walls?

Karsen: Yeah, just the walls. It was just white in here, basically. We sat with the elders, and started discussing how a tipi is set up. We started getting the idea of wanting to set up a tipi, and have different murals on the side, so we can connect more to our own land.

For a lot of people, Chief Mountain is just a mountain. For us, we have our own ways and stories of it, and it's kind of ceremonial—sacred. And we also have different places for the ceremonial uses of it, and we wanted to implement it into our school so that students recognize it.

A lot of people on-reserve, they don't recognize that. We do have things like this, and they don't understand a lot of our ways. That's how we set up this tipi; we discussed with the Elders on how it was set up, and how a teepee works. That's how we got the idea of it.

The buffalo hide, we actually came up with that too, because the buffalo was our main resource back in the day. We wanted to bring that here to symbolize that this was what we survived on, and what we used back then. Now we just wanted to show what it symbolizes, and the meaning of it to our people—especially our bundles and our smudge, and the setup of—that's what we really learned from our Elders.

Shirley: Did the math class do the measurements as well? So everybody helped?

Karsen: Yeah, and the art class painted the murals, so it was all a student-driven initiative to start this.

Shirley: Have you met the Elders before?

Karsen: Yeah. I'm also related to all of them.

Shirley: Okay. Did you know them as Elders, though, or as relatives? Have you always had the teachings from them?

Karsen: Well, mostly from my grandpa. I knew him as a relative, and also with his teachings, growing up—especially since he went to a residential school. So I guess I didn't really hear so much of it, though I did see it at the Sun Dance.

I was a very much a part of it [the Sun Dance] and growing up in that kind of setting; but I never really engaged myself into it completely. Since my grandpa and my grandma went to residential school, they were really kind of closed-off about that, and they wanted their children to be raised in a way where they have to adapt to the new ways.

By getting an education, that's what they really pushed them towards, and that's what I was pushed towards, and so I didn't really learn more of our cultural ways, and with Harriet and Leroy [the Elders], I just knew them as Elders, and Rose, too.

But now, coming in here, we actually use the elders in classes. If we're talking about a subject, like in my biology class, we came in here and we'd get their perspective and their teachings, and put it in as a part of our curriculum, too. That was really interesting. The elders weren't really prepared, but I think one of the teachers was just like, "Let's try it." But it ended up working out, right?

Mike: How long have you had the Elders-in-Residence Program?

Shane: [This is] our second year.

Karsen: Since we developed this, they've been a part of it right from the start. Because it was new, we needed their teachings. We just found the money, and just kept [inviting] them. Then this year it was just put right into the budget, so then they're here until we run out of the money.

Shirley: Tell me, do you use the smudge?

Karsen: Well, not really, me personally. Growing up, I've always been around smudge, but I never really actually knew how to use it. I know a lot of students who do come in here to use it, but I remember for my pig dissection, I got grossed out, so I just came in here to smell the smudge, because it's just more relaxing.

It calms you down just to come in here, and just chill out, I guess.

Shane: I like how you said that some kids don't even know. They think this is only ceremony, right? They weren't raised up like that, because they were told—and our Sun Dance, our traditions, it was only for privileged people—but that's not how it was. Actually, our Sun Dance means a gathering of our people to rejuvenate for another year. It doesn't mean that it was just a ceremony.

It was a place that everybody gathered once a year to reunite and get through the year, and helping through stories and teachings and stuff like that. That's what [the Sun Dance] meant, but kids don't know that, because of the church told them it was bad. That God is the only way of living, which is the same as the Creator. In every culture it's the same thing. It's just that people identify as what they believe in, right?

And ours isn't different. Every little thing, like the smudge, it's a place where when we pray, the scents are going up to the Creator with our prayers. And in church, they do the same thing, you know? So just stuff like that, a connectedness in everything we do. Some people don't, because, remember how I said we're taught how Indians, we're not equal. So they think that our way is just savagery.

But it's basically just the same thing; it's just that we always talk about these things. I think it was actually Leroy that told me. If you go to a Chinese person—same thing, they burn incense, right? We see where that comes from. Let's go and let's pray, but if it was our way, it would be totally different, because we're not seen as valid.

That's why it's harder for our people to recognize that our ways and how we existed is how we're going to succeed, and that's where our kids are stepping back in. This is what we need in order for us to get where we're going.

Karsen: And not necessarily labeling instead of knowing our ways.

Shane: But that's true, she said this ain't a religion. This is how we existed. This is our everyday. I was reading this thing—Facebook is my newspaper—we were talking about playing hockey with nearby Mormon schools, they don't play hockey on Sundays because they go to church on Sunday. So the rest of the kids on the team can't play on Sundays. So if there's a game on Sunday, they have to forfeit that game, which wasn't fair to the other kids that were on that team that weren't Mormon.

There's this big discussion, and they were saying, "Well, don't you guys pray?" We pray every day. It's not a thing where just go to church on Sunday. We pray every day, to every living thing—we pray. This is our source of life. We pray it's going to continue being out there so that our people could go back to an understanding of how they can help themselves through that.

Grass, the grass growing. Kids, when they come in to my office, they always tell me. What's the first thing you see? Oh, the grass is dead. It just shows where their mind and their body and their spirit is. I used to think so too, but when I look outside, I always think, "Green grass coming up."

I see something underneath that is growing. That's what I think about kids. I don't see that dead grass out there. I see something that's growing. And that's what our elders were teaching.

Shirley: Can you even imagine the school without the tipi now?

Karsen: Not really. It would be kind of weird, just having an open room. We didn't even use this room for anything. For the longest time it was just—what was it? I don't know, before.

Shane: It was basically like this. It was supposed to be like this. But we were like, "But why won't we have couches here—"

Shirley: But you had no circle?

Shane: Kids weren't utilizing it, you know? It was left open for them to come in and sit, but...

Shirley: People can come in here now, any time they want?

Shane: Yeah. They get permission from their teacher, and they come in; or even just if they need a private space. Someone would come in and sit there, and she had to regulate herself, and she had to do it somehow.

When we get sick and start walking out on a teacher, and the teacher doesn't understand that, [the student isn't] doing that out of ignorance, she's just doing it because she doesn't feel comfortable in that situation. When [the teacher] came into the room, and she grounded herself in feeling comfortable, she understood that this is how it's going to help.

See, kids are coming back to our way of life, just even that little bit.

Shirley: And there was nothing like this in your off-reserve school?

Karsen: No. Not a lot of our cultural ways were utilized, and not a lot of it was talked about. We did have prayers, like if we had some sort of assembly or a big thing, we would have a prayer. But some of the First Nations students who attended didn't understand what the prayer meant. And after our prayer, we put our hand to our heart just to take in that prayer and accept it, but not a lot of students need that.

When I did it, that's like growing up. That's when I knew what to do. And kids would ask, "Why do you do that?", and it's like, "I don't know, I've just always done it." But coming here, learning that, if she's taking in those prayers, accepting it, and just being thankful for everything. That's what it kind of symbolizes.

We didn't really have chances to express ourselves by going to different conferences, and seeing different things about it. Before, I wasn't really aware of issues relating to mental health, and coming here it's been talked about a lot more, and they even have a program that teachers take part in, in the Brain Institute.

They're trying to understand our students, and where they're coming from, whereas off-reserve, they're just like, "It's your problem," you know? Because I'm assuming, growing up, that when [the interviewer] went to [their] school, did you have very close relationships where you could phone [your teachers]?

We actually call a lot of our teachers by their first names, too, and talking to my friends who go to school off-reserve, they're like, "How could you just talk to them when they're formal?" I even have their phone numbers and Snapchats. It's just building a relationship and being able to trust one another. I find that students off-reserve don't have that closer connection to their teachers.

Shirley: Who made the decision for you to go to a reserve school?

Karsen: It was my decision, because I was going through a lot. I was actually bullied by one of my teachers. It was a bit of a funny thing. So, that was a really tough decision for me, because I grew up going to school off-reserve. That's all I've really known.

I just wanted to go to a school where I'm not going to be judged because of my skin color, and I'm not going to be put down for it, and it'd only make me try harder, because there's lots of kids who are just like me. And going to school off-reserve, they didn't really have an understanding of how I grew up, and they didn't know where I was coming from, so I just couldn't do it anymore.

Having that sense of not being able to belong somewhere, and when you don't feel welcomed, you don't do very good in life. It's just a known fact, because if you don't feel comfortable, how are you going to be able to be productive? I just made the decision of coming here, because I knew a lot of people, and a lot of my cousins were here. I knew a lot of the teachers too. So, I just thought, you know, what the hell? Might as well just go.

We also have a good sports programs here, and I'm very into sports, so that's another reason why I came here. Coming here was probably one of the best things I've ever done, because I get to be a part of things like these. Being able to good in a smaller setting really helped me a lot, personally. Having teachers that you can to go to talk to when I'm having problems and to have them be more understanding is very helpful.

Having our own elders' room is pretty cool, because we get to connect in ways where we could understand from an older perspective and a more traditional sense. That's who we are. It's just cool. I don't know.

Shirley: So, you've decided to build a solar panel?

Karsen: Yeah.

Shirley: Tell us about that.

Karsen: Well, in my science class at my old school, we were learning a lot about it. In my biology class, we were talking about different ways we could use less fossil fuels, and climate change, and trying better alternatives to use, and I thought of solar panels, because in China, a lot of places are switching to solar panels for their energy use, and they're saving lots of money from it, too. Especially with them being such a rich country.

Alberta is really high-altitude, and since we have a lot of sunlight here, we actually get a lot of the same sunlight that California does. So with that, we'd be saving a lot of money [with a solar panel].

It's just beneficial for us especially, and coming from a school out here that's really open, and we have a lot of these open fields that we could utilize for solar panels and saving a lot more money. With that money we're saving, we could put it into using things to build a greenhouse, so we could plant our own resources. And with that, we could even begin to sell it, like our own produce, and with that produce we could be getting even more money, and we could start having more programs for our school—that's just my thinking of it.

Shirley: So this year that will be your project?

Karsen: Yeah, and we're working with our lands department.

Shane: There's a coordinator that does [work on] climate change around the reserve. She wanted to see if the kids were interested. They brought in our staff to see if anybody was interested in helping with that project or wanted to get the grant money to do something. She didn't tell us why. It was just basically for climate change. And we were asked, "Why don't you get your leadership kids involved?"

She came to give a presentation and the students thought of the solar panels and the energy efficiency [to talk about] if we didn't have all the lighting and stuff that uses "generated" energy, I guess you call it, to get our school going. That came from them, and that's what we really see here. We've got to start listening to our kids, you know?

We can have degrees, but we've been doing that for ages, and we're in the same place, you know? The issues are still there. We have to listen to our kids, and understand where they're coming from, so then we address it from their perspective.

Shirley (to Shane): Listen to our kids. You started listening. That's pretty strong social action, isn't it?

Interview with Karsen Black Water and Shane Wells, Kainai High School, Kainai Nation, Standoff, Alberta, Canada

Chapter 24

"We've Been Here, and We're Still Here, and We're Still Going to Be Here for Thousands of Years"

Interview with Students of Kainai High School

Editor's Note:

The following is a transcript of a conversation between Kainai High School's student leaders, Shane Wells, Shirley Steinberg, and Michael Holden. The group met in December 2017 to continue sharing their experiences as change-makers and as Indigenous Youth. Karsen Black Water, Carley Shot Both Sides, Jordan Weasel Head, Keyshaun Mountain Horse, and Kiara Blood are keenly aware of how other people perceive them, and how national issues like Missing and Murdered Indigenous Women (MMIW) unfold in their daily lives. This conversation highlights how this group of students reconciles these challenges with their desire to make a difference a world where their views are not always welcomed or understood.

Shane: Shirley is writing a book, and so she wants to get everybody's input on what we're doing, keeping in mind that we're still doing the mental health stuff. We're still doing that. ... This project is still going, and then our new project would be the climate change research we're doing. Okay?

Shirley: We're writing a book, and the book is about activists—youth activists, youth that make a difference—and it's a book that's going to go to schools and to teachers about how kids can do stuff more than that people think they can. Your work is an absolute example of youth activism, that this [tipi] was created and made in such an amazing way. The [tipi] is amazing, because this is was inspired by youth. And in talking to the Elders the other day, this has created a whole community space that never existed in most high schools.

But today, it'd be just nice to talk to you more, and to ask you how you came about this idea, and maybe just other things that you'd like to do; things that you think, as youth, that you can make a difference about.

There's an idea that people think they know what's good for the reserve and what's good for First Nations people. What you said the other day made so much more sense to me as a teacher, and it's to understand that when we are in our own environment like you've created here, you've created a home environment which is also a traditional environment. It's a spiritual environment. It's so much about being Blackfoot—right in this spot.

Back to your mental health issue, one of my questions is how does this environment, contribute this idea of home and tradition? Do you think that contributes to mental health?

Karsen: Being First Nations, and being a Blackfoot woman, I have a statistic of being murdered or going missing, and having to live with that every day, it's like I could go into town and have a chance of being taken. It's just realizing, to accept who you are; and I'm proud of being a First Nations woman, and being from one of the biggest reserves in Canada. Everyone has their own identity, and we just all need to find a belonging, and I have a belonging of being Blackfoot. When you don't know who you are, or you don't have a belonging to somewhere, you get lost, and you feel that disconnection from society.

And so, it does contribute a lot to mental health, because people who say "move to Canada," and come from another country often struggle with the world, because they don't have that group, and they don't have that strong sense of feeling. And bringing it to here, and having other students try to find their sense of identity as a Blackfoot is important. Because in a big world like this, it's easy for us to get lost, and just finding out who you are is really good for you personally, and also good for our culture, especially. Because if we don't recognize who we are, we lose [our culture].

Shirley: Keyshaun, you were nodding your head. What were you thinking when she was talking?

Keyshaun: Mmm.

Shirley: You agreed when you shake your head when she said about losing yourself.

Keyshaun: Well, yeah. That happened to me a few times. "Who am I? What am I doing here?" Stuff like that. I slowly started to actually listen to our culture, that's when I was like, "Oh, so this is where I come from. These are my ancestors." And you know, just learning more about our culture—

Karsen: It just built you up as a person?

Keyshaun: No. … When you're living in the modern world, but you have a different culture, a different setting and everything, you tend to feel lost in both worlds. You don't know which one you go to, but once you learn about the other one that you know nothing about, it's a little bit better, because you have a sense of belonging. You know how you would feel. You would feel more at peace with yourself. Something like that. So, that's pretty much why.

Karsen: Especially since on our reserve, we face a lot of troubles with abusing alcohol and drugs, and those weren't part of our culture. We all lived in harmony, and we always practiced our beliefs, and always tried to make ourselves better as people, and come together as one. We have a lot of people in our community that don't recognize that, and as a young group of people, we want to make a difference for people in our school. So, that'll lead on to the next generation of leaders, because as everyone says, we're the future, and we just want to continue on advocating for us as Blackfoot people.

Shirley: Right. Now, you're a senior; you graduate in five months?

Kiara: Yeah.

Shirley: How do you feel about that?

Kiara: I'm excited and sad at the same. I'm quite ready to leave high school. It's a big stepping stone for me.

Shirley: Do you feel like you're going to be a grownup, or do you feel like a grownup already?

Kiara: I kind of feel like a grownup already. But, I'm excited.

Shirley: What do you want to take from this particular experience of, maybe not finding your heritage, but rediscovering and embracing your heritage? Do you have plans to take that into the future?

Kiara: Yeah. I really want to go into university for anthropology. That's based on human culture. I really want to go into that, and just finding everyone's own identity and different cultures and race, and my own; because I'm a Blackfoot person.

Shirley: That's really great. It makes a real difference, doesn't it? What about you, Jordan? What are you thinking of? You're in grade 11?

Jordan: Well, Karsen was right about we all have that—where, being native women, we have that [fear of becoming] missing and murdered. We went to Missoula last week for basketball and when the girls on our team went to the mall, we were all worried about the girls walking alone because they were scared that they were going to get taken by somebody. Everybody was worried about Karsen, because she went off on her own.

That's all they worried about. Scared that somebody on the team might go missing, and they shouldn't have to be worried about that going to a shopping mall. That's all they were worried about, is somebody going missing.

My friend Alyssa was in American Eagle [store], and the lady there kept watching her when she was walking around. That was really sad, because other girls in there had their bags and they weren't getting watched. But Alyssa was, and she didn't want to go into the stores anymore. She stayed by the teachers, and that was really sad to hear she had to go through that. It was sad to know that all the girls were worried about was each other going missing, when they could've been having fun at the mall, and just enjoying it.

Every time we go for sports games, we have a talk about getting racial comments, it's very sad that that's all we have to worry about. I think this project would be really good. What we're doing is really good, because there are a lot of kids in the school that are struggling with drug addictions and alcohol addictions and they're just little kids. I still think of them as little kids, and that they need to enjoy [school]. But they're just worried about getting drunk and getting high when they should be enjoying this high school experience, and knowing what they want to do with their future.

[Kids should come] to school for sports and these clubs to have fun, and not be worried about going home to get high or get drunk, or worrying about if they're going to have food to eat at home. They should just be worried about coming to school and getting good grades, and not having to worry about what they're going to do after school. They should be just worried about having fun and having all these experiences at school.

Karsen: Just adding on to that: there's a big misconception with being First Nations, because people think we're set up to fail, and from the beginning of signing treaties and coming up with the Indian Act, which was set up so that we would fail. In our school, as a group, we want to show that there's more to our lives than just what's expected of us, and we want to show that we can grow as people together, and go on to bigger things. As my dad always says: high school isn't everything. There's a bigger world out there, and we should explore it.

We're trying to show people that, in our own school, and hopefully in our community, drugs and alcohol aren't always the first thing to turn to. We can all get our education, and we can all go for jobs, and we can just beat that misconception of us being drug addicts.

Shirley: You're in charge of it. I think that's important. You refuse to let that label hit you.

Karsen: We're just not trying to be stereotyped, and beat the expectations of us.

Shirley: No, and why should you?

Karsen: Yeah.

Shirley: You're (Carley) the quiet one. What are you thinking about?

Carley: About Karsen and Smokey. How people kind of lose their self in this world, especially when they're a different race. That's happened to me a lot of times, and I'm still going through it right now. I just think that what we're doing here is really good, because it's helping me find myself, and I feel accepted now, somewhere. Like I belong here.

Shirley: Belonging is important, isn't it? I mean, it's hard enough in the world to be a woman, but to be a minority woman or man—and I say "minority" when it's sort of ironic, because you come from a people that was the majority—and it's very clear that that has made an incredible difference in your lives.

In fact, when I lived here in the 70s, before Kainai was its own school division, and it was under Cardston School Division. There was no native voice; the native voice was an announcement, "The Indian bus is late." That was the native voice. And the kids from here had to be bussed for hours and hours, starting at 5 in the morning, to get to off-reserve schools—especially for high school.

Now, by the changes in the Band (Blood Tribe), and the Band taking over the responsibility of its own empowerment, this has made a huge difference. The fact that now, 20 years later, you're sitting here in your own environment that is from your heritage, and created by your own decisions—to me it's huge. It's very huge because this is not the ability that First Nations people used to have, and certainly not during the residential-school days, when they were beaten if they even spoke Blackfoot.

As much as they seem like small steps, these are enormous, and to hear five of you talk like you're scholars and academics, using language that's just incredible. Your knowledge of what's happening is phenomenal. I think I'm looking at five leaders, and I think that's incredibly cool.

When you talk about missing and murdered women, it's just mind-blowing that if your family gives birth to a baby girl, and that could be her possible future, especially in Western Canada. We're in a world that that makes no sense. Michael, maybe you'll tell them the experience you had just walking by yesterday, as a White man from the East, and what you saw at the cafeteria.

Michael: I was going home, and as the university medical team is there, and campus security is there, and some paramedics are there, and some cops are there, and I'm thinking...

Shirley: At the cafeteria?

Michael: The cafeteria. Why are they here? What do they want? What's happened? Usually, when there's that many people, something bad has happened, but they're talking to this guy who's sitting there in the cafeteria. Just sitting there. Just this Native guy sitting inside. Public cafeteria, middle of the day, and they're asking, "Why are you here, what are you doing here?", like he's causing some sort of trouble, like he's been fighting or something. He's just sitting there. Ten people, one guy.

I can't wrap my head around why is this the response. If he needs some help, fine, help him. He's just sitting there.

Shirley: It's like you were talking about what happens when you go into a store. The Syrians I work with have very similar stories. The Black Canadian students I work with have similar stories. That idea, if you don't look like us [White], then for some reason that puts a sign on your back that you're suspect. It's pretty incredible, especially going back to the fact that this is your land. That cafeteria is on Treaty 7 land.

It's something to take with you, and the fact that you want to do good work—always talk about this. Don't let the White man silence you anymore, like he has for so many generations. You have teachers, and you have Elders now, and your own voices to become significant for you to make a difference now as high school kids; but then you walk out—and just that idea of telling the truth. Naming the truth is very important. It's something we're not able to do very often.

Karsen: Yeah. Living in Canada, which is known for its multiculturalism and diversity, and we have a Charter of Rights and Freedoms that's supposed to protect us as individual groups, and being able to express who we are and not be discriminated against. We go through so much racism throughout our lives. I'm only 16, and I've faced racism since I was in grade 1. As long as I can remember. It's hard. I'm not going to lie.

The other day, not too long ago, I wanted to go to the shopping mall, and I get a text from my mother and my brother. This long Facebook post about indigenous women going missing from the Lethbridge Park Place Mall. I go there all the time, but I could go missing, and it's ridiculous. Being able to get the chance to go speak in front of the Alberta Legislature, it's a really big opportunity for me just to represent everyone in my school, and the Blackfoot people, especially the women.

To me, that's really important—sorry, I'm kind of emotional, because to me it's really important. Especially what [the book editors] are doing, in giving us this opportunity, like social change, and even you guys recognizing that what society is doing is wrong. We want to make a change, and coming here together, I'm really thankful for that. I'd like to thank you guys for listening to us and giving us this opportunity to do better; not only for us and our school, but the rest of Canada and the world. That really means a lot, so thank you.

Shirley: Well, I think we're pretty humbled by being around you, because you're the heroes. We're just the teachers, you know?

Michael: When Shirley asks "so what's important and why are you doing this work?" And to hear the first things you talk about are murdered and missing women; every day, every trip, when you just go to the mall. And that you have to have a talk about how to be safe and watch for being taken and those sorts of things. It's exactly what you said. "I'm a kid. I'm 16. That's not something I should have to think about." It has been sort of shrugged off for people who don't have to deal with that... "Oh yeah, that's something people talk about."

Karsen: That actually happens. I've been followed around in stores so many times.

Jordan: You just get used to it.

Karsen: Yeah, it's just a reality. I have people watching my every move, and I can go into a store, and I could see a White person walking, and immediately the person goes up to them and asks them "How are you doing? What do you need? Do you need any assistance?" and I've been in there for five minutes, ten minutes, maybe. All they can do is stare at me, and not even offer me so much as a simple greeting, or ask if I need any help. It's just feeling kind of shunned, and it's hard, I guess.

Shirley: Have any of you ever been in a place that you would not be recognized as Native? That you could be Spanish, that you could be Syrian—have you ever had that experience?

Keyshaun: Yeah, I have.

Shirley: Have you?

Kiara: In Toronto, that's all.

Keyshaun: For some unknown reason, I've gotten called Asian once.

Kiara: Yeah, I did get called Asian.

Shirley: Asian? So, it's still a racial concept? So, it's sort of like, "White, and everybody else" kind of thing?

Keyshaun: But the main ones that they mostly go to is either Pakistani or Spanish, but they'll call these other words too.

Karsen: Some people don't realize that First Nations people still exist. In social studies, we were talking about how our one teacher was in another university. I think an East Indian person came, and he was crying in and in tears. He said that he was taught that we were all killed off, and that no First Nations existed.

Even some people who lived in Canada—land that belonged to the First Nations—and we've been here for over thousands of years, and not even recognizing that this is where we come from. This is the land you live on, and I think a lot more people need to recognize that First Nations do still exist. We've been here, and we're still here, and we're still going to be here for thousands of years.

You're living with us now in our area, you should be able to accept it by now. Especially how to go through things like this, it's just kind of dumb.

Shirley: It's like a human insult in a sense, and actually, in talking to you, I think next year will be really interesting to try to focus more of our groups, getting you introduced to other groups of non-White kids. Because I think certainly, everyone has different issues, but it's so interesting that just by color of skin and hair, that people can treat people so differently.

I think what your voices are doing, too—because I'm hoping a lot of our work goes out to other youth—is the lack of knowledge about missing and indigenous women. In fact, there's even groups in Canada that say it's just not true... you know, talk to the families and find out how true it is. But that idea of being able to talk to other youth and let non-Native youth know what it's like to have this hang over your heads at all times. It's pretty phenomenal.

Shane: I think listening to them talk about Syria and Pakistan and these people—they have a place of origin, right? They have a country where they come from. But as First Nations people, this is not our country anymore? This is not our country. This is Canada, and we don't have that place of origin. That's why we're not as the same playing field as anybody else.

If we, say, go to meet these people, another race; but we still don't have that place of origin, how do we teach our people? Yeah, we can say this is our language. We know, as First Nations people, that other people say "No, no, this is Canada," but any time we try to succeed, we're oppressed by a group of people that will continue to do that, regardless of if we can have the highest standards. We can have somebody that's sitting in Parliament, sitting as a Prime Minister, but we never will, because we're not seen as the same as anybody else. They had a Black president in the United States, because they had a place of origin. They're accepted for who they are.

Shirley: That's very interesting.

Shane: But we don't have that, right? So we're confined to this little piece of land—

Shirley: Where they put you. It's not like your people say, "Oh, we want to move out to here, and this is where we want to be," but it was like being herded. It was a buffalo jump and you didn't have to fall to the bottom. You just got pushed here.

Shane: Yeah. That's why I really like listening to our youth, because we have tried as adults, as our tribal leadership, our national leadership, but nobody is listening. And they're saying, like you said, "Oh, well, you're just saying that just to get attention." But these are girls that are living with this every day.

Like Karsen said, they talk about it on the National News. "But it wasn't recognized." No it was not recognized, but if you had something that happened to another race, it would be recognized, and people would say, "Okay, let's get some Red Cross money in there to help these people," and have these [First Nations] people say "Yes, we were given an apology by the government to say 'yes, we apologize for putting your people in residential school.'"

Shane: What are you going to do, right? It's like me walking by and saying "Sorry, you can't act like that." What is it going to do? We're still being oppressed by a government that will continue to do that, because they don't want to recognize that wherever they are situated in Canada, that [land] did not belong to them. That [land] belonged to First Nations people, and [the settlers are] just visitors. But us, we have to fight for that place of origin. This is our own land.

Shirley: In your own land, you have to fight for the origin. This brings up a question: when you've been to events—I would imagine you've been where they've done the land recognition thing? Like, we're standing on traditional territory, then they do a land acknowledgment. Have you heard this before? If you go to an event that's Canadian. Have you heard this?

Shane: You know how they call it. They'll say that [they would like to] recognize that we're on Treaty 7 land or Blackfoot territory.

Shirley: How do you feel about that when you hear that? I'm very interested.

Karsen: My mom works at the Lethbridge College. What she's trying to do, and what her group's trying to do is to have more Blackfoot recognition at their institution. Going there–and even by going to other events—it's like "Oh, this is Blackfoot land, Treaty 7 territory." Where did this happen, and all this. It's like, "Yeah, it is, but do you know the history behind it. Do you know what happened out of those treaties?"

People don't think it still affects us to this day, but I have to show a card [a tribal status ID card]—it has numbers on it—to say that this is who I am. That number says I'm Native, and if I don't have that number, then I'm just like any Western Canadian citizen. We're the only people in Canada, and in the world, who has to have a status card to say, "This is the group we're a part of." It still affects us today in trying to show that we are First Nations, and having other people recognize this is our land. We could say it, but you have to learn the history behind it even before having to say it. Just knowing the knowledge of it.

Shane: The correct history. Right.

Shirley: So, the land recognition isn't quite the correct history?

Shane: Yeah, because like I say, the government says these are our people. We were talking about it a couple days ago, they're putting into our social studies curriculum the content of First Nations people. But, they don't recognize that each Nation is a nation of its own. We're not all one. We have different values, from the people down east, to the people down west. It's a whole new thing, and are they going to teach that to Canadians? No, they're not.

Karsen: In our social studies class, we're talking about nationalism, and we talked with the elders, and I asked a question: "What does the word nation mean to you?" For them, they said that when they were signing the treaties, they were against the word nation because we're in Blackfoot territory, and before all this land belonged to us. We could move our tipis to the West, to the North, to the East, to the South, anywhere we like. We had Crow people, Stony people. Many groups of people, but we all knew our place, and the word nation to us, kind of broke us apart. Because when we were put on reserves, we weren't begun as a nation. We were Blackfoot. That's who we were, and still are today.

But the words nation, nationalism, kinda separates us from each other. The government's main goal was to put us as nations on reserves, to split us apart so we could have these feuds between one another, when really, we came from the same place. We're talking about a term called "contending loyalties" and for us, it's like, are we First Nations, or are we Canadian? Who do we identify ourselves first as?

For me, when somebody asks, "Oh, where are you from?" do I say I'm from Canada? But I'm First Nations, and they're like, "Oh, you're Canadian." Yeah, but I'm First Nations, and then I'm a Canadian. Us talking about that and talking about patriotism and being proud of where we come from, but—yeah we're a part of Canada, but we live on reserves. So, should we be vouching for "Yeah, this is reserve land. This is where we come from," or do we say, "This is Canada, we come from here?"

Canada isn't the country. It's recognizing we still need to come together and recognize these individual groups, and especially First Nations. To be patriotic not only for our country, but also ourselves, and talking about the recognition of our own land. I wonder what our land would've been called if settlers didn't come here and name this land Canada. If we grew up in a world where North America still belonged to Indigenous people, what would we be called? Would we be a nation, or would we be just us? I'm curious to know. If there was only a time machine. I guess we just have to live with what we have now.

Shirley: So, when you hear "land recognition"—I'd like to say that before we start, in fact we have one that we have to supposedly read, and I don't usually read it. I usually just say that we're on land that was stolen from the natives. So, when you hear that, it never talks about the history. Why do you think it's read? Why do you think that? Why do you think people do this recognition?

Keyshaun: I would say just for appearance; like, at least they did something, instead of just being—

Karsen: "Oh, we recognized them. That should be good enough."

Keyshaun: Yeah, that should be good enough. You know, but you didn't see any change happen after that. After that it was just the same thing. After Reconciliation. Maybe a few changes, but I don't know.

Shirley: In Australia, they gave an "I'm sorry" to the aboriginal people about 15 years ago, and people started wearing T-shirts that said "Sorry." It's funny when you see the word, and there's such a silliness, isn't there?

Keyshaun: Yeah. I don't know if you know about the 150th Canada Day. I don't know if you've heard from other Aboriginal people. They didn't feel like they wanted to celebrate it, because it was pretty hurtful years for them, way back then. Even just maybe a few days ago.

Karsen: It's kind of funny, because we've been here for more than 150 years!

Shirley: That's a really good point. It just occurred to them that it's 150 years.

Keyshaun: Well, we did go to see the fireworks, because fireworks are fireworks; but we just couldn't actually celebrate it.

Keyshaun: That's all we did, but we didn't actually say, "Oh yay, 150. Yay this."

Keyshaun: Yeah. Me and my grandma and all my other parents, we were just like, "Oh, it's 150. Okay." Something like that. It was just a little hard for my grandparents to actually say, "We're proud of this 150," because I could tell you a lot of stories about my grandma. She's gotten hit with a ruler across the ear, and that still makes me really sad, because no kid should go through that.

I was at this one camping place; I can't remember where it was. I think it was up North, and someone said, "Let's say something like we're from different cultures," or something like that. And there's a few comments that went around that were just like, "Okay."

But then, I think one of the people got it wrong, and it kind of stirred me up. It was some guy talking, he was a drummer, a singer; and I was listening. He was there, and there was one comment that said, "Why don't you just get over it." And there was a Native person said, "Oh yeah, this is what people say. Why don't you just get over it?"

I think they misinterpreted that, they said, "Yeah, why don't you get over it?" and that guy, he broke down. Me, I was in the front seat. I was shaking. I was mad, because how can I get over this? It affects me, even though it didn't happen to me—it's someone I love a lot: my grandma, my grandpa. They were the ones who raised me, literally; because my mom, my dad, they're out drinking.

I was with my grandma and grandpa. They converted to Christianity, but that didn't change their language. They still wanted to keep that, because a part of them felt like they still needed to keep our culture going. My grandpa was traditional, my grandma, she read the Bible; but they still loved each other, and they respected each other's ways.

My grandma would go to these pow wows; but my grandpa, for him, he felt like he didn't belong at the Sun Dances, because he was with a Christian woman, and I think that kind of [took] him a little far away. I kind of felt bad for him, because he loved our ways. He enjoyed it. Everything about it was awesome to him. It's still hard for grandparents, because they were in residential school.

For me, I knew that they loved me, but sometimes they'll always lash out and stuff. But either way, they still love me. For my grandpa it was tough love, but I learned to understand. At least I'm still getting something from him. I went off-topic there, but—

Shirley: No, no. You're good.

Keyshaun: As I said, he would say the same thing I'm saying. [That I] can't forget about [our ways]. So I stood up. I said, "How could someone say that?" It's not even directly to me, but it hurts me still. It hurts me so much to hear someone say "Why don't you forget about this?" you know? We can't just forget about it.

All the stories my grandma and grandpa have told me, they stuck with me. It does affect me a little bit, emotionally and mentally. When I joined this program, I realized this is something to do instead of being out there drinking. It actually did stir away from that. I'm 100 percent drug- and alcohol-free. But anyways, it's a little bit more [than that]… well, I do have issues and stuff. We're not all perfect.

That comment that someone said to me—or not to me, but to [my grandpa]—still affected me, because it still generalized our people.

Note from Shirley:

Speaking with the youth at Kainai High School has been an extraordinary experience. After they initiated and created the tipi in the high school, they have continued to use it, for visits, speaking with the elders, to smudge, or to relax and reflect. They are in the midst of creating a solar plan for their school. For many years, the schools on the Reserve (in the US called a Reservation) were controlled by a nearby town, Cardston. Over thirty years ago, the Band (organization, in the US called a tribe) determined that the students and general population would be better served if the Band controlled the school division. Kainai is a unique example of a school which acknowledges the need to encourage Blackfoot culture, language, and ways of knowing along with the curriculum of the province. Students are able to attend school on the Reserve, as the students we are working with do, but can opt to attend a school off the Reserve. In order to attend the Youth Forum, the students and teacher travel three hours each way to Calgary.

Interview with Karsen Black Water, Carley Shot Both Sides, Jordan Weasel Head, Keyshaun Mountain Horse, Kiara Blood, & Shane Wells, Kainai High School. Kainai Nation, Stand Off, Alberta, Canada

Afterword

My Story

Assmaa Yassin

Editor's Note
Assmaa Yassin is 19 years old, she gave this presentation on March 9, 2018 for International Woman's Day, after learning English for less than two years.

As-salamu alaykum…this is how we greet each other in Arabic. My name is Assmaa Yassin. I am 19 years old. I was born in Syria, in the city of Damascus…a city now in ruins as the war continues to destroy my country. In 2013, when our home in Quneitra was bombed, my family was forced to move. Over the next nine months we moved several times to find safer places to live. We ended up on the Syrian side of the Golan Heights. At this point my mother decided for our safety we should move to Lebanon. My father elected to stay behind to protect his widowed mother, he would join us later in Lebanon.

My mother, my four sisters, my youngest brother, and a male cousin set out on foot to search for transportation. After a day's walk we reached an area close to the border where my mother paid a driver to take us across to Lebanon. Sadly, the driver took our money and would only take the two male passengers. The women were left behind to fend for themselves. After begging and pleading my mother found a kind gentleman from Aleppo, who agreed to take us to Damascus. This to me is a great example of the persistence and will of a woman to protect her family. Ultimately, three days later with the help of an uncle we made the crossing into Lebanon. We left Lebanon and were so happy to come to Canada, sponsored by the Hillhurst United Church in February 2016.

Life in Lebanon was harsh and we had little by way of safety and security. However, one of the very fortunate things that happened while I was in Lebanon, was that I got to meet Malala Yussifi. The Malala School for Girls was opened and I was able to volunteer with her group. The first time I heard Malala speak, she opened my eyes to the possibilities of girls to get an education, and even more importantly she introduced me to the concept that "women and men" are equal and have the same right to education and other freedoms. Education is important to me, and I would like to become an archaeologist and because I am in Canada this is a real possibility. If I still lived in Syria I would probably be married by now and have one or two children and there would be no easy way to continue my education. Meeting Malala was my first step towards overcoming my fear and opened a door for me to look forward to the future with strength and confidence From Malala I learned that every person has talents that he/she must explore. All of this insight has made clear to me the importance of women's rights. Malala is a wonderful role model for all young women, she is teaching us to defend our rights, and not remain silent. I am proud to be here speaking about Malala and am thankful for having met her.

The dictionary defines rights: as privileges that cannot be taken away by governments, institutions, and others. Among these rights in Canada, are freedom of speech, freedom of the press, gender equality, and freedom of religion. While these rights are Human Rights, I have learned since coming to Canada they are also the rights of everyone in this country, without exception. This past year there has been a very vocal female movement to bring attention to women's rights especially in the workplace. Women have been speaking clearly and loudly in groups such as "Times Up" and "Never Again." These voices are demanding to be heard so that in future women in Canada and elsewhere , will not face discrimination, verbal abuse and harassment as they have in the past. Imagine how enlightening and liberating this is for a young women of my background. I am aware that our Prime Minister is an avowed feminist and is working hard, advocating for women's rights, gender equity and equality. As a newcomer to Canada this makes me very happy.

Who would have thought four years ago that I would be in a new country, speaking in public about women's rights on International Women's Day? CERTAINLY NOT ME, but life is full of surprises and opportunities.

Shokran.

Assmaa Yassin, Calgary, Alberta, Canada

Printed in the United States
By Bookmasters